IN MY PRIME

Also by Ellen Sue Stern

I DO
I'M HAVING A BABY
I'M A MOM
STARTING OVER
LIVING WITH LOSS
RUNNING ON EMPTY: Meditations
    for Indispensable Women

IN MY PRIME

ELLEN SUE STERN

A DELL TRADE PAPERBACK

A DELL TRADE PAPERBACK

Published by
Dell Publishing
a division of
Bantam Doubleday Dell Publishing Group, Inc.
1540 Broadway
New York, New York 10036

Library of Congress Cataloging in Publication Data
Stern, Ellen Sue, 1954–
    In my prime : meditations for women in midlife / Ellen Sue Stern.
        p.   cm. — (Days of healing, days of change)
    ISBN 0-440-50596-8
    1. Middle aged women—Prayer-books and devotions—English.
2. Menopause—Prayer-books and devotions—English. 3. Midlife crisis—Religious aspects—Meditations. 4. Devotional calendars.
I. Title. II. Series.
BL625.3.S74   1995
242′.643—dc20   94-44168
                                                                        CIP

Printed in the United States of America

Published simultaneously in Canada

August 1995

10 9 8 7 6 5 4 3 2 1

FFG

To my friend, Rachel,
whom I met at age nine
and plan to play with at age ninety

ACKNOWLEDGMENTS

As always, I give great thanks to my friends and family who have been such a source of love and support in the writing of this book. But above all else, I owe a debt of gratitude to the incredible women in midlife who are writing on this topic, courageously speaking out about the challenges of ripening, and who have been an incredible inspiration as I personally enter this stage of life.

INTRODUCTION

I began this book convinced that that topic had absolutely nothing to do with me. As the mother of two children, aged ten and thirteen, I could barely relate to the idea of menopause—it seemed light-years away!

Lo and behold, I discovered that, in fact, midlife is exactly where I'm at. When I celebrated my fortieth birthday I had entered this brand-new stage of life. There were a number of insights that made me realize that this book was personally relevant: As I watched my daughter, Zoe, enter adolescence, I saw that the two of us were bookends on either side of the maturing process. As I began to take stock of my life—and make new and different choices—I perceived this stage as a period of reflection and discovery that comes of being able to look both backward and forward with a certain measure of experience. And I recognized myself in the beautiful writings of women in midlife, who speak of the increased confidence, savvy, and wisdom we gain as we move into our forties, fifties, and beyond.

So I got excited! And I saw myself as part of a community of women coming into our prime. My images profoundly shifted from my perception of midlife as a time of decline to seeing it as an incredibly wonderful passage into a far richer stage of life. I've learned that midlife offers a tremendous opportunity for self-examination and spiritual growth. That, to sum up the sentiments of my friends and sisters, this is a time when we give ourselves permission to play, to be gutsy, outrageous, and honest to the core, that, to put it simply, we get to be ourselves, in all our beauty, in all our glory.

And so I give you this book with gratitude for having had the chance to grow. May it help you do the same.

The woman who is willing to make the Change must become pregnant with herself, at last.

—URSULA LEGUIN

Pregnant. It's a word used to describe the ripe, expectant state of a woman carrying a child.

Yet there are so many ways to be pregnant. Filled with ideas, hopes, plans, and dreams. Pregnant with the anticipation of a new relationship, career, or other exciting changes in our lives.

But it is one thing to be pregnant with a child and yet another to be pregnant with ourselves. As we enter midlife, we are bursting with our own ripeness, coming to fruition, realizing our potential, readying ourselves for whatever lies ahead.

Pregnant with ourselves, we begin an internal, utterly compelling journey toward rebirth.

AFFIRMATION: I am filled with anticipation.

The menopausal woman seems to be the most glibly dismissed of modern beings.

—MAGGIE SCARF

The two words that leap out of this quotation are the words *glib* and *dismissed*.

Being "glib" means that we laugh at, scorn, or ridicule our feelings. "Dismissed" means we ignore, diminish, or even disdain the importance of the passage we are going through.

We mustn't allow anyone to minimize the importance of menopause. When this happens, it's important to stop and educate. To say, "This is a meaningful life passage. Let me tell you how it's affecting me."

And just as we shouldn't permit others to trivialize menopause, we must be sure to name and claim the value of this experience for ourselves. The first step is simply to say:

AFFIRMATION: I respect the importance of what I'm going through.

You can always go on a diet. But what do you do with your face? You can't go to NutraSystem for your face.
                                                    —SAURA MORRIS

I don't know whether to laugh or to cry reading this quote. She's right of course; we can't go to NutraSystem for our face, although enough lotions, peels, and surgical procedures abound to transform our aging skin at least as much as our overweight bodies.

There's something funny, yet also sad, about our frustration with our aging face. What should we do with it?

We should treat it with love and respect. Instead of figuring out how to lift, liquefy, or lessen our wrinkles, let's try to see our aging face in a more positive light. It is, after all, the only one we've got.

AFFIRMATION: My face is my history.

> *The cruelest myth is that menopause is a time in a woman's life when she goes batty for a few years.*
> —GAIL SHEEHY

Feelings of distraction, distress, or emotional chaos are natural and appropriate responses to going through change.

Having these feelings doesn't make us a basket case. We needn't downplay these emotions, nor do we benefit from "checking out" and checking in to the local psychiatric ward until we're back to our "old" selves.

As we go through the Change, we can also work on changing our own and other people's perceptions of the process by getting rid of words such as *batty* and replacing them with words like *intense. Emotionally charged,* even *volatile* are better than *crazy* for describing this period of time.

AFFIRMATION: No matter what anyone says, I'm not crazy.

There is no bar mitzvah for menopause.
                                        —PAULINE BART

First, it should be bat mitzvah, which is the correct name for the customary Jewish ritual ceremony for a thirteen-year-old girl's coming of age.

But whether we say *bar* or *bat,* the point is—there *should* be a formal ritual to celebrate the change of life. We're beginning to understand the value of symbolism in marking this profound life passage. In increasing numbers women are creating "bat mitzvahs" for menopause: crone circles in which midlife women light candles, dance, drum, and in other ways ritually celebrate the Change.

Just as it's important to ritualize our first period, our first sexual experience, our first pregnancy, we can give menopause the reverence and respect it deserves.

AFFIRMATION: I will make a point of marking this passage.

> HOT FLASH: Light a candle for each
> month's missed period the first year.
>
> —NAN O.

This is the first of weekly hot flashes—news, information, and tips from women in the front lines
of coping with menopause and midlife issues.

Here's how one woman, Nan, a fifty-two-year-
old graphic artist, ritualized her passage into
menopause. She says, "Each lit candle reminded
me to stop, notice, and think about what it meant
to be entering this new stage of life."

Another woman, Stacy, created a ritual using
watercolors representing the different aspects of
menstruation she had experienced over the
years. Georgia affirmed her menopause by invit-
ing three friends in their forties and fifties to join
her for a weekend camping retreat.

In their own way each of these women cre-
atively celebrated their Change.

Ritual is highly individual. Now's your chance to create an imaginary ritual as a way of symbolizing your Change of Life. Let your fantasies run wild as you complete this worksheet.

My midlife ritual would include:

CREATIVITY

It's at fifty that you really come into your maturity as an artist.

—Judy Chicago

For Judy Chicago, famed feminist and creator of the art piece *The Dinner Party,* coming into maturity is manifested in her identity as a visual artist.

But we can substitute so many other words for *artist.* Some of us come into our own as mothers, managers, athletes, attorneys, or anything else that defines our primary focus in life.

Ultimately we are in a process of coming into our maturity as individuals, having reached a stage of inner certainty and quiet confidence in who we are and what we have to give.

AFFIRMATION: For me maturity is manifested in my increased ability to . . .

There we were, the ten of us, bitching and moaning,
revealing shared fears.

—ERICA LANN CLARK

Here's to midlife support groups, sometimes referred to as
crone circles or fan clubs. Here's to the bitching and moaning that helps us get it all out with other women coping with
similar side effects. Here's to sharing fears, questions, problems, and remedies with laughter and tears. Here's to cama-
raderie. To sisterhood. To all the good reasons for starting or
joining a support group with other women who can offer so
very much. It may be the one best gift you give yourself
right now.

**AFFIRMATION: Sharing my fears makes it easier to
cope with them.**

FRIENDSHIP

> *It's very important to have another woman friend or*
> *friends who are the same age or a little older.*
> —CHARLAYNE HUNTER-GAULT

It's a little like having a tennis partner who has a bit more experience, the tiniest edge that pushes you harder to play your best.

The same is true in every arena of our lives. We need peers—other women who have achieved at least the same if not greater wisdom—as beacons and guides.

Perhaps that's exactly what a good friend is: someone like us, with us, and in some significant way a few steps beyond.

AFFIRMATION: It's good to have somebody to help light the way.

MONTH ONE   **DAY ELEVEN**

It is sad to grow old, but nice to ripen.
—BRIGITTE BARDOT

Old and *ripe*. How very different these two words sound.

Imagine for an instant a pear that has sat too long in the bowl on the counter. It's wrinkled and mealy; its wooden taste barely evokes the sweetness we remember.

A ripe pear, in contrast, green, shiny, with tender skin and juicy, succulent meat, fills us with pleasure. *Ripe* means ready. Perfect. All the way there.

Which is what we are on the way to becoming.

AFFIRMATION: I am ripening in the nicest possible way.

There has to be a letting go of the clinging remnants of any reproductive fantasies.

—MAGGIE SCARF

As mothers midlife presents us with an opportunity to continue letting go of our children—of a time when they were younger and needier, of a time when our energies were higher, our focus on them central to our identity.

And those of us who have remained child-free—for reasons of choice, biology, or destiny—now have the opportunity to let go of our fantasies of motherhood as we accept the end of our reproductive capacity. In the process we may find ourselves struck by feelings of loss, saddened that motherhood is no longer an option. And so we grieve, which is essential to moving forward. As we relinquish fantasies, we gain a firm footing in what the future holds.

AFFIRMATION: I am ready to let go of what has been and what may never come to pass.

HOT FLASH: Spend time with babies.

—Kim B.

Kim, a fifty-year-old mother of two college-age daughters, says she got her weekly "baby fix" by baby-sitting a friend's newborn. Hannah, age forty-eight, whose son was recently married, says she volunteers in a preemie nursery as a way of getting to hold and cuddle the babies she misses so much.

There are lots of ways to enjoy the sweetness of babies without turning back time or having another one of our own. If this is something you miss, do something about it.

How are you feeling about letting go of your growing children or living without children in your life? Is there anything you can do to spend time with, play with, or nurture other children you know?

I can:

When did the boys I once clung to start losing their hair?

—JUDITH VIORST

I vividly remember the first time it hit me that I was getting older. I was sitting at a party and caught a glimpse of my then-husband, Gary, across the room. I was shocked to see that he was almost completely bald.

Where did that gorgeous wavy head of hair go? I wondered. Had this happened right before my eyes, without even noticing? And, if *he* was balding, I must not be twenty-five anymore!

Our mates—and often our friends—reflection can be a striking blow to our own self-image or a glorious affirmation of our own emerging maturity. Their aging makes ours that much more visible and real. It all depends on how we look at them—and how we look at ourselves.

AFFIRMATION: I can look in the mirror and see myself in the present.

GRATITUDE

*If we could sell our experiences for what they cost us,
we'd be millionaires.*

—ABIGAIL VAN BUREN

In midlife we take stock of our economic status along with
everything else. We may be grateful for financial security that
affords us luxuries as well as the chance to be charitable. We
may count ourselves lucky to have the basics, or we may
struggle to make ends meet.

Whether we are affluent or struggling, planning vacations
or scratching lottery tickets, we all have one thing in common: a wealth of experience that money can't buy. Although
we can't take it to the bank, we *are* millionaires in terms of
life experience—and our bank accounts get bigger each day.

We can count our wealth in lots of ways: in the friendships, knowledge, and wisdom we've gained through forty or
fifty years of living on the planet.

AFFIRMATION: I have so much.

It is a good idea for women to count their ages, not by years, but by battle scars.

—CLARISSA PINKOLA ESTÉS

In her best-selling book, *Women Who Run with the Wolves,* Estés describes battle scars as "proof of the endurance, the failures, and the victories of individual women."

Battle scars are the stuff of character—the physical, emotional, and spiritual remnants that come with having fought the good fight, learned the hard lessons, struggled through the trials and tribulations that have presented themselves through the years.

Our battle scars *are* our birthdays. We count the years: 40, 50, or is it 1,082—by the experiences that have shaped our character and determined who we are today.

AFFIRMATION: I am _____ years old in experience.

*A time of letting go of our waistlines, our vigor, our
20-20 vision, our fantasy that Paul Newman will finally
leave Joanne. . . .*

—JUDITH VIORST

Although I've been myopic since I was eleven, and frankly
Paul Newman has never made *my* Top Ten list, it's true that
each of us has different hopes, dreams, and fantasies to relinquish in our middle years.

What are yours? Going to medical school? Running the
marathon? Having an affair with that gorgeous hunk you keep
running into at the bookstore, who's triggered more fantasies than you care to admit?

As we mature and become more aware of our gifts as well
as our limitations, we sort through our fantasies and decide
what's doable, what's risky, what's worth fighting for, and
what's never going to happen, except perhaps in our wildest
imagination.

We find a way of balancing our dreams with reality, putting our energy into what's essential, into what's likely to
give us the most in return.

**AFFIRMATION: I am ready to let go of my fantasy
of . . .**

MONTH ONE   **DAY NINETEEN**

I felt my first hot flash while standing in line at the hardware store.

—KAREN N.

This quote reminds me of an exercise we do in Expecting Change workshops, when participants share the story of the moment they found out they were pregnant.

Now here's the same question with a new twist: Where were you when you experienced your first hot flash? Or when you first became aware that you were entering menopause?

Think back. It may be two months or two years ago. Can you recall how you felt? Were you scared? Excited? Unsure of what was happening inside you?

AFFIRMATION: I remember feeling . . .

HOT FLASH: Wear men's oversized tank tops to bed.

—DIANE K.

This tip comes from a forty-seven-year-old librarian, who says, "I put away my sexy teddies and nightgowns and bought dozens of cheap cotton undershirts that are lightweight and easy to slip out of when you're dripping wet."

In other words make comfort your priority. If you're tormented by hot flashes, forget vanity and opt for wearing something cool, washable, and with lots of ventilation for those nights when you're not sure of what's ahead.

Changing your wardrobe to accommodate hot flashes is but one way in which you might currently alter your routine. What other ways are you changing your habits or lifestyle in order to ease menopausal symptoms?

   On the next few lines write down any tangible changes you are currently making:

1. _____
2. _____
3. _____

GOOD-BYES

Good-byes are sad, no matter what the promise of tomor-row is.

—Janet Leigh

I've used this quote before. In books on motherhood, saying farewell as each and every day we let go of our children a little bit more. In books on divorce, in affirming the importance of allowing ourselves to grieve our loss as we rebuild our lives.

And now, in midlife, we have more farewells to bid: Good-bye to the younger woman who has slipped away with time. Good-bye to our capacity to conceive life, to our monthly connection to nature's cycle, to a time that cannot be recaptured and must be put to rest.

In turn, as we say good-bye, we are more fully able to embrace all that we are becoming and all that lies ahead.

AFFIRMATION: Good-bye. And hello.

My children have a higher power, and it's not me.
—ANONYMOUS

Regardless of our love for our children, our lovers, our friends, at a certain point we need to relinquish our hold, trusting that their lives are unfolding according to plan, with or without our divine intervention.

For those of us with children, this is especially important to learn as we enter midlife. As our children become teenagers, adolescents, and young adults, we remember that our loved ones have their own path to follow—and that we must love them enough to let go gracefully.

AFFIRMATION: As I let go, my energy is freed up to focus on my own journey.

CHOICE MAKING

*Full maturity is achieved by realizing that you have
choices to make.*

—ANGELA BARRON MCBRIDE

Every life passage presents us with the challenge of making
new choices. Choices that reflect our cumulative knowledge,
wisdom, and clarity gained through experience. Choices that
reflect our most deeply held values and beliefs. Choices that
affirm our growing self-respect and willingness to risk all in
order to create what we need.

The capacity to make clearer, wiser, more self-affirming
choices may be one of the best markers of maturity. We
know who we are. We know what we need. We're willing to
act confidently in our own best interests.

**AFFIRMATION: Confident choice making is an ac-
quired skill.**

This crinkly turkey crepe under my chin. Hanging so loose I could have pulled it back six whole feet, I thought.

— "DORIS" QUOTED BY GAIL SHEEHY

Some days our aging visage appears so dramatically distorted that our laugh lines may as well be two feet long, our skin may as well be leather, our sagging chin may as well hang down to our collarbone.

What really matters is how we see ourselves and how we feel about what we see. Some days we're pleased by our reflection; other days looking in the mirror is nothing short of painful. Just as we struggle with "fat days" or "bad-hair days," when we fall short of our ideal, other days we feel fine—or even great—about the physical transformations of midlife.

The trick is to accept what we see without feeling bad about feeling bad. And to hope we have at least enough good days to balance out the rest.

AFFIRMATION: I will try to keep a balanced picture of how I look right now.

TRANSFORMATION

*We become not harder with age, but softer, not as bitter,
but more gentle.*

—Marianne Williamson

That depends. We've all seen older women who appear hard
and embittered, their pain and disappointment deeply en-
trenched in the furrows of their brow, their countenance a
chronic frown that makes us cringe and want to look away.

Other older women take our breath away. Their face is a
map of life well lived. Their eyes contain a sea of sadness and
joy. Their smile is a wise, knowing one; their carriage, regal
and dignified as an oak tree.

We become harder or softer with age depending on how
we deal with our struggles. The challenge is to transform
our pain into compassion, humility, and wisdom.

AFFIRMATION: I will not let life get the best of me.

HOT FLASH: Find an older woman to learn from.

—RHEA T.

"When I turned forty," says Rhea, "I met a woman in her late seventies who became my friend, mentor, and spiritual guide."

For some of us that older, wiser woman may be our mother. Or our grandmother. Or the woman down the street with whom we chat while she's pulling weeds in her garden. What matters is to learn all we can from women who have been there before, for they are beacons along the path.

Each of us has questions we wish we could ask of an older, wiser woman. What are yours? List four questions you have about aging:

1. _____
2. _____
3. _____
4. _____

Now list at least two older women you're willing to turn to for guidance:

1. _____
2. _____

The idea of aging has been difficult for me.
—LINDA LEONARD

These simple words get right to the heart of the matter.

For many of us the concept (or idea) of aging is as difficult or even more difficult than the reality. What we envision is alarming; we fear infirmity; loss of our faculties; erosion of our appearance, our independence, our earning power; and the ultimate loss of the people we love.

But the reality may be far more manageable than our worst fears, which may or may not materialize. We can't predict—or control—our destiny. We *can* harness all our best energy to envision a hopeful future rather than fixating on worst-case scenarios that may never come to pass.

AFFIRMATION: I will expect the best.

MONTH ONE   **DAY THIRTY**

Taking joy in life is a woman's best cosmetic.
                                        —ROSALIND RUSSELL

We extol the virtues of exercise, diet, even sex as an antidote to the natural physical decline that accompanies aging.

But what about joy? Perhaps happiness, joy, and, yes, ec-
stasy, are the most effective cosmetics of all. The times we
feel happy and hopeful, gloriously right with the world, create an inner and outer radiance, beyond what any mascara
can do.

What brings you joy? What are you actively doing to make
joy a part of your daily beauty regime?

**AFFIRMATION: Today I will notice the moments I feel
joyous.**

Youthfulness, fragility, and vulnerability are the essence of sexual attractiveness in a woman.

—MAGGIE SCARF

Wow! If these are the three ingredients of sexual attractiveness, then all of us past the age of twenty may as well just pack it in.

I, for one, beg to differ with this limited definition. Maybe it's because, as I'm turning forty, my youthfulness is quickly fading; I'm tougher, stronger, and far more resilient than I was twenty years ago, all of which I celebrate!

Perhaps it's time to redefine what makes a woman sexy and attractive. How about qualities such as maturity, strength, confidence, and power, just to name a few? Because what truly makes for a sexy woman is a combination of strength *and* fragility, innocence *and* wisdom, power *and* vulnerability—and the confidence to manifest all of the above in a genuine way.

AFFIRMATION: Here are two adjectives I'd use to describe female attractiveness:

1. _____
2. _____

FREEDOM

Still to this day, I never did know why fishing and menstruating were mutually exclusive.

—STEPHANIE ERICSON

They're not. As the Tampax commercial featuring a woman on horseback implies, having our period is no reason to put a halt to our activities, no matter how strenuous.

On the other hand there's something to be said for fishing, horseback riding, or just about anything else without worrying about our period.

The freedom to come and go as we please—unhampered by Tampax and menstrual cramps, sans the accoutrements or other attendant aggravations related to our monthly flow, is one of the side benefits of menopause for which we can clearly be grateful.

AFFIRMATION: There are some real pluses to no longer having my period.

And then, not noticing it, you become middle-aged and anonymous. No one notices you; you achieve a wonderful freedom.

—DORIS LESSING

Freedom. It's a word that comes up again and again for women in midlife. We experience freedom from constricting roles and expectations we've traditionally placed on ourselves. We enjoy freedom from the monthly pressure of menstruation and birth control. And, here, as Doris Lessing says, we experience freedom from the sexual advances and overtures we have experienced in younger years.

It *is* liberating to be less noticeable, to be able to be less self-conscious. But only when it's *our* idea, our desire to fade into the background. Some days we enjoy the increased anonymity. Other days we throw on a bright red shawl, a purple hat, or smile at strangers *just* to get a response. We get to choose. And *that's* freedom!

AFFIRMATION: I can be as subtle or as flamboyant as I choose.

LOVEMAKING

In bed my husband no longer looks for my G-spot. Now he looks for a dry spot.

—GAYLE SAND

From all accounts, finding a dry spot in the soaked bed of many menopausal women *may* be easier than locating that elusive, infamous G-spot that's been the subject of countless talk shows and women's magazines.

There's no question about it: The annoying wetness that often accompanies hot flashes can put a real damper on our sex life. So what can we do about it? Here are a few tips from wetter-but-wiser women:

- Wear all-cotton pajamas to bed
- Make love in the morning *after* taking a shower
- Sleep in the other bedroom so that you're rested and refreshed
- Develop your sense of humor

AFFIRMATION: Our sexual relationship will survive. Meanwhile I will focus on other forms of intimacy.

> *Nature gives you the face you have at twenty. It's up to*
> *you to deserve the face you have at fifty.*
>
> —COCO CHANEL

Most likely Coco was referring to cosmetics and clothing as the "price" we must pay in order to keep up appearances as we age.

On the contrary, I vote for happiness, vitality, and serenity. Although even at thirty-nine (and holding) I'm buying more classic clothing and slathering Oil of Olay on my face before bed, I still know none of these efforts compare with the physical beauty reflected on the face of a mature woman who's comfortable and at peace with herself.

Ultimately nothing we put on our face—or our bodies—can substitute for what's in our minds and in our hearts.

AFFIRMATION: I look like who I am.

HOT FLASH: Get a massage.

—Eleanor V.

Better yet, get regular massages! It's a great way to relax, replenish ourselves, and to ease any aches and pains we're experiencing during menopause.

This is one treat worth splurging on. (If massage is beyond your financial means, contact a local massage school; students often offer free sessions as part of their training.) Or just ask your mate for a backrub! Sensual stroking is good for your spirit!

How are you nurturing yourself right now? Are you getting massages? Facials? Taking hot, candlelit baths in which you soak, luxuriate, and let your worries wash over and out of you?

Self-nurturing only happens when we make a commitment and are sure to follow through. Make one commitment now to do something that helps you feel rested and replenished:

   I will:

MONTH TWO   **DAY EIGHT**

> *From age eighteen to thirty-five, a girl needs good looks.*
> *From thirty-five to fifty-five she needs a good personal-*
> *ity. From fifty-five on, she needs good cash . . . from*
> *thirty-five on, she needs good cash.*
>
> —SOPHIE TUCKER

Actually we all need all three: looks, personality, and plenty of cash, no matter how old we are.

In midlife, more than ever before, we are motivated to do everything possible to enhance our appearance through diet, exercise, wardrobe, and rest. More than ever before we need to express our personality, unleash our sense of humor, and hone our unique sense of style.

And cash doesn't hurt either. Having money to spend, to save, to share, is an added bonus that makes a tangible difference in our lives.

AFFIRMATION: I promise to spend a little extra on myself right now.

The climacteric means the end of apologizing.
—GERMAINE GREER

Climacteric—the clinical term for menopause—*can* mean the end of apologizing, which women do day in and day out, often unaware that we're even doing it.

We apologize for being too busy, too demanding, too intense, too sensitive, even too apologetic! It gets crazy, especially since there's nothing to apologize for in the first place.

We do it because it's what we've been taught; it's a way of being "nice," of not rocking the boat, keeping other people happy, and getting their approval.

Stopping the pattern of constant apologizing doesn't automatically come with the transition into midlife. We have to make a real and concerted effort to notice every time we say "I'm sorry" instead of saying to ourselves:

AFFIRMATION: It's okay to be who I am, to want what I want, without apology.

APPRECIATION

I look at my body and think, "Wow! I have hips! This is a woman's body!"

—ELENA FEATHERSTON

Before you say, "Yeah? Just take a look at *my* hips!" consider the spirit of this woman's words.

She looks in the mirror and revels in her roundness, in her singularly female curves, softness, and fullness.

She looks through woman's eyes at woman's body and says, "Yes. This is beautiful. This is pleasing."

I am inspired to take another look, through my approving, accepting, and appreciative eyes that can clearly see:

AFFIRMATION: I am a woman. Wow!

Age does not protect you from love. But love, to some extent, protects you from age.

—JEANNE MOREAU

It's true. A woman "in love" appears relatively ageless. Her eyes are radiant, her skin aglow with anticipation. There's a spring in her walk, a sparkle in her smile.

To be sure, as we age, we are no less vulnerable to the difficulties of love—the disappointments and sorrows, the losses and the lessons. But we give and receive with greater ease that comes of having loved before, only this time with more wisdom and maturity. If anything, being in love is a greater gift the older we get.

AFFIRMATION: I'm never too old to feel in love.

PRODUCTIVITY

> It was terrifying to lose my quintessential power to make life.
>
> —Erica Lann Clark

We experience loss—and perhaps confidence in our value—as we contemplate the hard truth: We can no longer create life.

Being able to conceive, to carry and give birth, for those of us who are mothers, was indeed a powerful way to make an impact, as well as a means of immortality.

By the same token, no longer being reproductive certainly needn't mean an end to our productivity. We continue to make a difference in a million different ways. Take a moment to name one way in which you are becoming more productive.

AFFIRMATION: I express my productivity by:

Women who are mothers feel the pressure to keep doing all the things their families have come to expect.
—CONNIE BATTEN

Whether or not we're mothers, we all feel pressured to keep up our Herculean efforts to do everything for everyone. Both at home and in the workplace, being an "indispensable woman" takes an added toll during midlife. As we race around overextended, we tend to eat on the run, skip our aerobics class, postpone our medical checkups, and stress ourselves out, which exacerbates menopausal symptoms.

If there ever was a right time to say "Me first," it's now. We must occasionally put others on hold and say yes to ourselves, even if it means renegotiating what we're able to give to everyone else.

AFFIRMATION: I'm not indispensable.

Here is the most fundamental and healing exercise of all—to breathe. Simply breathe.

Remembering to stop what you're doing and take a few cleansing breaths will help keep your mind, body, and spirit in balance. Begin now. Breathe deeply. Notice how this gentle process occurs.

Did you know that it pays to be zaftig after menopause?
—DORIS BIRCHAM

First—a definition. *Zaftig* is Yiddish, meaning "voluptuous, curvy, with a little extra padding in all the right places."

Unfortunately the extra pounds rarely settle in the place we'd have picked. We wouldn't mind a bit more cleavage; instead we get cellulite. We could stand some weight (or preferably muscle) on our upper arms, but instead it lands right smack on our thighs.

So we count calories in order to stay on the thin side, in order to be attractive and sexy. But here's the rub: The thinner we are, the more likely we are to suffer the effects of osteoporosis. As we age, we may need to add a few pounds to our "perfect weight," trading vanity for sanity as a way of tipping the scales in our favor.

AFFIRMATION: I like to weigh _____, but I'm willing to weigh _____ in order to help prevent osteoporosis.

I think it's lovely and wonderful to make it into your forties.

—Maxine Hong Kingston

A new twist on midlife: How fortunate to have made it this far. To have lived forty or fifty years, hopefully in fairly good health. To have experienced so much and still be here to talk about it.

So often we feel discouraged in light of our aging. Perhaps there's also reason for celebration. And gratitude. For being among those lucky enough to have made it this far—and still with so much left to look forward to.

AFFIRMATION: I count myself among the fortunate.

Robert Redford's lines of distinction are my old-age wrinkles.

—Jane Fonda

We're harsh in our judgments of ourselves and other women. We equate beauty with youth; we see women's attractiveness as temporal, whereas aging men are considered sexy and attractive well into their seventies.

And it's not just Robert Redford. There's Sean Connery, Woody Allen, and Marlon Brando, just to name a few. Whereas women are expected to conform to a universal image of beauty, balding, wrinkles, even sagging jowls are excused in men.

Consider Kramer, star of *Seinfeld*. Or Lyle Lovett. Can you imagine what would become of Julia Roberts's career if she looked anything like her husband, who's so homely, he's cute?

Yet older women are every bit as attractive as older men. It's time to drop the double standard so that we can see how beautiful we really are.

AFFIRMATION: I can change my conditioning.

SELF-ACCEPTANCE

We grow neither better nor worse as we get old, but more like ourselves.

—MARY LAMBERTON BECKER

Perhaps we should alter this sentiment to read, "We grow either better *or* worse as we get older, depending on how well we like and accept ourselves."

This is one of the great challenges facing us in midlife. We honestly confront who we are—our identity, our values, what we've made of our lives. We either make peace with where we're at *or* we become bitter and resentful over mistakes, misfortunes, and missed opportunities.

If we celebrate ourselves, giving thanks for the mixed blessings, for every single experience, better or worse, that's made us who we are, then we continue to grow into the wonderfully unique person we are.

AFFIRMATION: I like who I am.

Cleaning your house while your kids are growing is like shoveling the walk before it stops snowing.

—PHYLLIS DILLER

What does housecleaning have to do with menopause?

Everything, depending on the age of your children, and how much you do or don't care about the mess!

Those of us with school-age kids—or beyond—celebrate new order as children clean their rooms (if we insist!) or better yet, move the piles to a college dormitory.

As mothers we have put up with the mess way too long, looking the other way until a time when we could finally create the sort of atmosphere we want.

Start now. Clean one closet. Throw (or give) stuff away. Have a garage sale. As we bring much-awaited order to our homes, we bring a certain measure of peace into our lives.

AFFIRMATION: Time to straighten up.

HOT FLASH: Create a space for yourself.
                                        —Maggie G.

When my friend Maggie turned forty, she created an "art studio"—a small corner of her living room where she could draw and paint at least two hours a week. Doing so required extensive negotiation and juggling in order to maintain her other responsibilities, but she was determined to see it through.

Virginia Woolf wrote of a "room of one's own," of the need for women to carve out a singular space in which we can create, dream, or do anything else our hearts desire.

The key is privacy. If you haven't done it yet, midlife is the perfect time to claim your own private space. It may be an office, a loft, or just any nook or cranny that's off limits to everybody else —that you can call your own.

Carving out our own time and space are essential for women in midlife. Having a "room of one's own" allows us to create without interruption, to retreat, reflect, and freely dream, even for an hour a day.

Where do you go in order to be alone? Have you created a space—an office, a den, a studio, or a comfortable corner in your home—that you can call your own?

If you haven't, make this promise to yourself:

I will carve out some time and space for myself. This is how I will accomplish it:

How old is middle age?

—ELLEN SUE STERN

Remember when middle age was twenty-five? Thirty-five? Ten years older than whatever birthday we were currently celebrating?

Perhaps middle age simply means being in the middle. The middle of what? The middle point of our lives, when we have as much to look back on as we do to look forward to.

What an ideal place to be. In the middle. Halfway between our past and our future. Old enough to appreciate what we have, young enough to count on so many more tomorrows.

AFFIRMATION: I am somewhere in the middle of my life.

One of the many things nobody ever tells you about middle age is that it's such a nice change from being young.

—Dorothy Canfield Fisher

My daughter, Zoe, is turning twelve. She's worried about boys, bras, braces, and all the other anxieties of adolescence.

I'm turning forty and I'm worried about boys (okay, men), bills, and whether this book will be finished by deadline.

I wouldn't trade places with her for all the first kisses that will never come again. Yes, midlife *is* a terrific change from being young. I celebrate the confidence, grace, and self-assurance of forty, even as I wistfully watch my daughter's coming of age.

AFFIRMATION: I'm grateful to be a full-grown woman.

The lovely thing about being forty is that you can appreciate twenty-five-year-old men more.
— COLLEEN MCCULLOUGH

Although there are lots of jokes, mostly derogatory, regarding older women and younger men, there's something to be said for sexy, experienced women in their prime.

For many of us libido may be more charged than ever; we're in touch with our bodies, unconcerned with pregnancy, enjoying lovemaking without dealing with monthly periods of pain and discomfort.

And as we enjoy our heightened sexuality, we may look at younger men, men our own age, or even older men through new, more appreciative eyes. Each age has its allure. In the prime of our lives we feel free to look at, lust after, maybe even seduce men of any age we happen to find appealing.

AFFIRMATION: Attraction has no age-related requirements.

I doubt I shall have affairs or bother my children when they are grown, for my real passion always has been writing!

—MICHELE MURRAY

Whether it's writing, biking, or birdwatching, midlife is a great time to recommit our energies where our passions lie.

If our children are growing or grown, we may have more time on our hands to pursue what makes our heart sing. Our work schedules may leave a bit more room to indulge in activities that bring balance and joy to our lives.

And if our schedules are stressed, all the more reason to consciously create time to follow our passions.

What are *your* passions? What are you willing to do to make them a priority?

AFFIRMATION: I am passionate about . . .

GRATITUDE

My forties were the best times I have ever gone through.
                                        —Elizabeth Taylor

I wonder if she said the same thing about her thirties? If
she'll say the same thing about her fifties, sixties, and seventies?

Let's hope so. Ideally each stage of life has its gifts and its
grief. Our forties can be a time of reflection, self-awareness,
and renewed confidence as we enter our prime. But then so
can our fifties, sixties, and seventies. Ideally every decade,
every year, every day of our life is the best one, containing
valuable lessons, pleasures, and challenges that make us say:

AFFIRMATION: Today is the best day of my life.

> **HOT FLASH:** This is the *best* time of your life!
>
> —NANCY F.

Why? Because, as Nancy, age fifty-four and a homemaker and community volunteer, said, "Since turning fifty, I'm a hundred times more peaceful, more comfortable with myself, and more appreciative of all the good things in my life."

This sentiment is overwhelmingly expressed by women in midlife. Most agree that being in our fifties and sixties is a period of greater fulfillment, during which time many of our hopes and dreams come to fruition.

The key is to be consciously aware of and grateful for the richness of this particular stage.

Time to count your blessings. What do you appreciate about being in midlife? What aspects of getting older are you grateful for?

List five things you appreciate about being in your prime:

1. _____
2. _____
3. _____
4. _____
5. _____

The mind of a postmenopausal woman is virtually un-charted territory.

> —BARBARA G. WALKER

Until recently menopause has been a taboo topic, rarely written about or spoken of, if at all, barely above a whisper.

We've had little idea what goes on during menopause, how it affects us, and what this experience means.

Welcome to 1995. A quick trip through local bookstores yielded the following gems:

The Silent Passage by Gail Sheehy
Is It Hot in Here Or Is It Me? by Gayle Sand
The Change by Germaine Greer
Women of the Fourteenth Moon edited by Dena Taylor and
    Amber Coverdale Sumrall
Coming into Our Fullness: On Women Turning Forty by
    Cathleen Rountree
On Women Turning Fifty by Cathleen Rountree

We are no longer silent. And we're learning so much from sharing our experience with one another.

AFFIRMATION: I needn't travel this road alone.

AUTHENTICITY

When I turned forty, I decided to make my statement. I started putting my hair in cornrows.

—Adjawa Jones

"My statement means that I am coming into myself as an over-forty woman." For Adjawa Jones, an African-American dancer, cornrows are a powerful statement of ethnic pride.

As we enter midlife, they are many ways of celebrating our heritage, be it letting our naturally frizzy hair go free, wearing a big silver cross around our neck, or donning the colorful sari of our native Indian ancestry.

Wearing our heritage proudly is yet another way in which we grow more fully into ourselves. It's a way of announcing to the world:

AFFIRMATION: This is where I come from.

Every woman can be an Oprah to someone.
                                    —MARIANNE WILLIAMSON

As "spiritual guru" Marianne Williamson, in her book *A Return to Love,* says, "Imagine what the world would be like if every woman showed support to at least one other woman, standing behind her in some way on the ladder of success?"

Midlife gives us the chance to be mentors. To extend our hand in wisdom and guidance to other women in the spirit of sisterhood.

Each of us has the power to teach. To inspire. To support other women by sharing the fruits of our experience.

AFFIRMATION: I am ready to be a teacher.

Menopause is the invisible experience. People don't want to hear about it.

—GERMAINE GREER

Too bad! Although, as Germaine Greer points out, for centuries menopause *has* been an invisible experience, women are breaking the silence right and left. We're talking about it, asking questions, and most importantly giving ourselves permission to count this experience as real, valid, and meaningful in every possible way.

Once we name our experience, it is no longer invisible, which is one more reason why we must continue openly and freely to talk about menopause, claiming its importance in our lives.

AFFIRMATION: We are no longer invisible.

After a woman passes menopause she really comes into her own.

—MERIDEL LESUEUR

Meridel LeSueur was eighty-two when she wrote these words, so I assume she meant our "golden years" (seventy-five and up) were a prime time when, as she says, we come into our own.

But each of us, at whatever stage of our climacteric, whether we're perimenopausal, menopausal, or postmenopausal, are somewhere in the process of coming into our own. Ultimately, ripening is a state of mind. It means coming fully into our self-assuredness, our confidence, our clarity as to why we're here on earth.

AFFIRMATION: My time has come.

I speak of the erotic as the deepest life force.
> —AUDRE LORDE

Whether we feel more sexual, less sexual, or asexual at this point in our lives, our eroticism deepens as we come more in touch with our sensuality, our spirituality, and our connection to all that is sacred.

We may experience heightened eroticism in many different ways: in the intensity of an orgasm, in our capacity to savor the silky sweetness of a newborn, in a newfound appreciation of erotic literature, or in the sensual pleasure of water against our thigh as we swim.

At its simplest, *erotic* means "alive." The more alive we feel, the more we awaken to the life force in and around us.

AFFIRMATION: I am open to eroticism.

*My mind is changing dramatically as I move toward
fifty.*

—PAULA GUNN ALLEN

I love this quote! Our minds *do* change as we move toward
fifty. Both our bedrock beliefs and more superficial opinions
evolve as we grow older, more sure of ourselves, stronger in
our convictions.

In some ways we may become more conservative in our
views on everything from politics to religion to recycling to
whether or not eating bran really makes a difference to our
health. And hopefully, at the same time, we become more
tolerant of opposing viewpoints, less rigid, more open,
aware that there are many ways of looking at things, all of
which can—and will—continue to change.

**AFFIRMATION: In the past year I've changed my mind
about . . .**

HOT FLASH: Fight for what you believe in.
—SARA E.

As our minds change, our values change, and we may become more dedicated to causes we're truly passionate about. For Sara, a forty-nine-year-old dentist, this meant becoming extremely active in her neighborhood crime patrol. As she explains, "In my mid-forties I started realizing that the only way to fight crime was for every single individual to do everything possible to make his or her own neighborhood safe. Since then I've made crime prevention my personal cause, to which I devote several hours a week."

This is yet another yardstick of midlife: Our changing beliefs are manifested in action.

How has your mind changed since you entered midlife? Are you more or less extreme in any of your beliefs? Have your politics undergone a transformation? Is there anything on which you've reversed your stand? Take a moment now to complete this sentence:

I've changed my mind about . . .

> *Age becomes reality when you hear someone refer to
> "that attractive young woman standing next to the
> woman in the green dress," and you find that you're the
> one in the green dress.*
>
> —LOIS WYSE

It can be a striking blow to our ego to realize we're no
longer seen as a "young woman," especially if our self-
perception hasn't caught up with reality.

I recently experienced this. A severe migraine headache
forced a trip to the emergency room. I was shocked when
the admitting secretary during her routine intake asked,
"Are you still menstruating?" I was taken aback. In the past
I'd always been asked, "Is there any possibility you're pregnant?" Apparently this no longer appeared to be an option,
making me feel acutely aware of my age.

However reality happens to hit us, it takes time to accept
that we are getting older, right before everyone's eyes.

AFFIRMATION: I will face reality.

MONTH THREE   **DAY NINE**

I will write myself into well-being.

—NANCY MAIRS

Writing *is* healing!

The words we put down in a journal, in a poem, in a letter to a dear friend help free us to heal and become whole.

And there are other ways as well. Some women draw, some garden. Some cook or sew or sculpt or run a mile first thing each morning before the sun's up, rain or shine.

What enhances your overall sense of health and well-being? Are you making sure to do it every single day?

AFFIRMATION: I take an active role in my own healing.

Maybe ourselves is an acquired taste.

—Patricia Hampl

Here's another way of saying the older we get, the more at ease we are within our own skin. We acquire comfort as we learn to live with ourselves—our quirks, idiosyncrasies, preferences, and tastes. We acquire confidence in our own inimitable style. We acquire trust that who we are is more than enough, that there is great value in simply being a human being.

It's just that it takes time—perhaps our entire lives—to acquire full acceptance of ourselves. Each day brings us a little closer.

AFFIRMATION: I am acquiring self-respect.

A woman's voice, soft and sultry, praises a night cream,
"Oil of Olay melts the years away."

—TRUDY RILEY

These magical marketing promises are both seductive and infuriating. On the one hand we're lucky to have access to skin-care products that help enhance our appearance.

On the other hand why should we *want* to melt the years away? Why erase our life's experiences, indelibly imprinted in the lines and texture of our skin?

Whether we welcome or resent these products, we may feel overwhelmed by the vast array of cosmetic counters in every department store. How do we know what to buy? (Ask for free samples.) How can we possibly afford them? (Products range from eight dollars to eighty dollars an ounce.) Most importantly, will they deliver on their promises?

Only time will tell. Better not to expect miracles, rather to invest in skin care that's affordable and that makes us feel good without melting the years away.

AFFIRMATION: I can care for my skin without trying to erase the lines of my life.

POSITIVE IMAGES

> *Thanks to Madison Avenue, the image of the menopausal woman was a matronly, sexless female whose shopping list included Polident, Metamucil, Geritol and Attends.*
> —GAYLE SAND

We must be living in the right decade!

Contemporary images of women in midlife include Jane Fonda, Lauren Hutton, Connie Chung, and plenty of other beautiful, sexy, vibrant role models, who seem light-years away from needing Geritol or Attends.

Still, these images are relatively recent. Years of conditioning have formed our collective images connecting menopause with the withering, shriveling, toothless old women we dread becoming.

It's time to update our images and focus on more positive, contemporary ones. Someone like you. And me. And all the other gorgeous women we see at the office, at the grocery story, in all likelihood right next door.

AFFIRMATION: I'll take another look.

HOT FLASH: Subscribe to *Lear's* magazine.
                                        —Faye M.

"I treated myself to a subscription for my forty-fifth birthday," says Faye, a single mother and chemical engineer. "It was easily the best gift I got!"

At the risk of sounding as if I'm "selling" something, I, too, give *Lear's* a big thumbs up. The magazine's tag line is "For the woman who wasn't born yesterday," and its pages are filled with images of beautiful, sexy, powerful women in midlife who make me, for one, feel excited about having reached this stage of life.

We can alter our images of aging by focusing on positive images. Here's how: Picture a half-dozen women in their forties and fifties whom you find attractive and sexy. You might imagine movie stars, public figures, or friends. Now write down the names of these women who help alter your image of midlife:

1. _____

2. _____

3. _____

4. _____

5. _____

6. _____

*Menopause has had a bad press. The bad parts have
been touted and the good parts have been kept secret.*
—ROSETTA REITZ

Negativity is a self-perpetuating cycle. The more we buy into
it, the more we're affected by the down-side of menopause.

Let's put some energy into considering the positives. And
into spreading the word. Here are some of the best things
women say about midlife and menopause:

- I'm mellower
- I'm more comfortable with my body
- My sexuality is heightened
- I don't care what other people think

Now it's your turn. Can you think of four more positive
things you can say about menopause?

AFFIRMATION:

1. _____
2. _____
3. _____
4. _____

CULTURAL DIFFERENCES

> *Women in Newfoundland are said to experience hot*
> *flashes as generally cleansing.*
> —DENA TAYLOR AND AMBER COVERDALE-SUMRALL

They say perception is everything, and maybe it's true. For example my friend Lauren insists she experienced labor contractions as pleasurable. Hard to believe, but then experience is highly subjective.

It helps to know that women in Newfoundland—or maybe the woman next door—may have a different, hopefully less uncomfortable experience of hot flashes and other menopausal symptoms. It helps to re-form our perceptions and open ourselves to another way of looking at things.

As our next hot flash washes over us, perhaps we can imagine it as deeply cleansing, as an opportunity for our body to release, purify, and restore balance and healing.

AFFIRMATION: Perception is everything.

*I work out so that my husband won't run off with a
younger woman.*

—ANONYMOUS

No matter how positive our self-image, how solid our marriage, midlife may provoke intense feelings of insecurity. Rational or not, we may find ourselves plagued by doubt: Does my lover still find me enticing? Is he turned off by my wrinkles? My stretch marks? My cellulite, which seems to have settled in for good?

Suddenly younger women appear threatening. Regardless of our feminist beliefs, we may feel competitive toward other women who may "lure" our mate, offering a quick fix for *his* midlife crisis.

It's okay to let these feelings surface. It's not, however, okay to obsess over them. If every younger woman suddenly seems like the enemy, it's a sign to get help. Help to create a healthier self-image. Help to get much-needed reassurance. Help to accept that while we're not getting younger, we *are* getting better in so many, many ways.

AFFIRMATION: I don't have to compete with anyone.

BEING PATRONIZED

The doctor kept saying, "Here, take a few drops of femininity, and then you can just run along."
—"DORIS" QUOTED BY GAIL SHEEHY

Being patronized is a particularly ugly form of glib dismissal. It's an insidious way of infantilizing and reducing women to a childlike, dependent state in which the doctor (father, expert, God) "takes care" of the problem rather than being in partnership.

If this sounds anything like your medical provider, run in the other direction! This sort of attitude is disrespectful on two counts, because: (a) none of us are looking for pills to preserve our femininity; and (b) none of us want or need to run along. What we *do* need is quality interaction with a doctor who respects us enough to take us seriously. It's the least we deserve.

AFFIRMATION: I expect my medical provider to treat me with respect.

I could be at greater risk if I was a red-headed, blue-eyed, freckle-faced, alcohol-drinking, heavy smoking, meat eating bedridden astronaut.

—GAYLE SAND

It's osteoporosis she's talking about, and it's small comfort to know that our genetic predisposition could be higher given a different mix of genetics, ancestry, lifestyle, and environmental factors.

Meanwhile we are who we are; we've done what we've done. We can't alter our risk profile or turn back time to change our past habits. We can, however, alter our destiny. We can change our diet, confronting our addictions; improve our exercise; and do everything in our power to stack the odds in our favor in the hopes of effecting a healthier future.

AFFIRMATION: I can take steps to improve my health and well-being in the present.

HOT FLASH: Quitting smoking dramatically decreased my menopausal symptoms.
—ELEANOR H.

If you like to light up, you might consider this revelation from Eleanor, a forty-six-year-old flight attendant, who, after trying everything, says, "Stopping smoking made my menopausal headaches virtually disappear and made a huge difference in the intensity of my hot flashes."

May be worth a try! Whether it's cigarettes, alcohol, chocolate, caffeine, or other addictive substances, midlife is a opportune time to quit or cut back in order to clean up our lifestyle and improve our health.

It's time to make new resolutions—ones you're willing to keep—to improve your overall health and well-being. What changes are you ready to make? Are you willing to alter your eating habits? Stick to a regular workout regime? Moderate your drinking? Get the Nicoderm patch?

List three positive changes you're ready to make:

In order to improve the quality of my health I'm willing to:

1. _____

2. _____

3. _____

SPIRITUALITY

What we hunger for is the other world, the world that sustains our lives as women.

—Clarissa Pinkola Estés

As women we are already deeply attuned to the "other world"—to the rich, spiritual source that nourishes and sustains us.

Menopause opens us further to the mysterious, mystical aspects of the universe. We become more introspective, more focused on ways of getting in touch with the cosmic forces.

Each of us expresses our spiritual longing in our own way. We do it through daily meditation. Through prayer. Through nature, music, dance, and any other discipline that renews our commitment to nurture our own souls.

AFFIRMATION: I move freely through different worlds.

MONTH THREE   **DAY TWENTY-THREE**

> *While I was thinking I was just a girl*
> *My future turned into my past.*
> —JUDITH VIORST

None of us know how many tomorrows remain. Each passing moment of our lives becomes the past in the exact moment we experience it. Which is why it's so critical to focus on the present rather than the past or the future. To awaken each morning, aware of the sunlight on our faces, giving thanks for those who are near and dear, living every single moment as fully as possible, is the best weapon against mortality.

Our past is behind us. Who knows what the future holds? Meanwhile we can savor each precious, present moment, grateful that we are alive.

AFFIRMATION: What matters is today.

EMPOWERMENT

Women don't have hot flashes. They have power surges!
—GAIL SHEEHY

This new interpretation of hot flashes are the words Gail Sheehy uses to introduce her recent best-seller, *The Silent Passage*. She heard this saying from a group of midlife women in California who met regularly to share their experiences of menopause.

How refreshing to think of hormonal surges as electrifying jolts, bolts of lightning, rushes of adrenaline, organic catalysts that energize and empower us.

This saying gets my vote for the universal slogan for menopause. Let's say it together:

AFFIRMATION: Women don't have hot flashes. They have power surges.

It just hit me that I'm too old to have a child.
—CAROLINE S.

Like the thud of a door closing, menopause forces us to face the finality of our choices regarding biological motherhood.

For those of us with children, we may regret not having had that third baby, not trying one last time for the daughter or son we really wanted.

For those of us who waited out of ambivalence, timing, or marital status, we see now that the decision is out of our hands. And those of us who are child-free, by choice or by destiny, may grieve the end of whatever shreds of fantasy remained.

Meanwhile we can still mother the children we have, extend ourselves to other offspring whom we love and care for and perhaps even the child we adopt—*if* we reach this crossroads and realize that now's the time.

AFFIRMATION: My nurturing takes many forms.

MONTH THREE   **DAY TWENTY-SIX**

If I take hormone replacement therapy, will I end up with breast cancer?

——MILLIONS OF MENOPAUSAL WOMEN

Ahh! The great Hormone Replacement Debate!

In the best of all possible worlds—and let's hope and pray medical research and technology get there soon—we could take estrogen to prevent heart disease and osteoporosis without risking breast cancer as a statistically frightening potential side effect.

It's not fair. And it makes the choices that much more complicated. Deciding whether or not to take HRT is tough. Take time and be sure to get a second and third opinion. Consult with a trusted physician and with women you know who can speak from their experience.

AFFIRMATION: Every choice involves risks and benefits.

HOT FLASH: Estrogen saved my life.
—MAYA T.

While this may be a bit of an exaggeration, devotees of HRT tend to be zealous in their appreciation of its benefits.

Here's what some supporters say:

"My hot flashes totally stopped."

"It took the crazy edge off my emotions."

"I felt more energetic."

"My libido shot way off."

Again it's not for everyone. But it's certainly worth serious consideration.

What do *you* know about hormone replacement therapy? Have you explored the potential benefits? The possible short- and long-term side effects? The various forms of administration? The financial costs?

Fill in the following worksheet in order to make sure you're up to speed on HRT:

1. Hormone replacement therapy is recommended for women who_____. It is *not* recommended for women who_____.
2. Potential benefits include_____.
3. Possible short-term side effects include_____.
4. Possible long-term side effects include_____.
5. Here are some of the various forms in which it is possible to receive it:_____.
6. HRT costs:_____.
7. My insurance does or doesn't cover HRT?___.

It's like the suffragists said, "Each one to tell ten to tell ten to tell ten."

—GLORIA ALLARD

Before there was *Ms.* magazine, before there were women's support groups and feminist marches, women spread the word—neighbor to neighbor, sister to sister, friend to friend. Whether it's the right to vote, the right to equal pay, or the right to *all* the available information on menopause and midlife, women continue to create an underground network of communication and support.

It's how we spread the word. At the supermarket, in the boardroom, in casual conversation, and in political caucus, we tell her to tell her to tell her until all women are hooked into this invisible, invaluable network of support and empowerment.

AFFIRMATION: I'll pass it on.

REFOCUSING

> *For me, it's the belated ability to ask, "What do I want to do" as opposed to what* needs *doing.*
> —GLORIA STEINEM

This definition of freedom, from Steinem's book *Revolution from Within,* is an apt description of yet another midlife shift. Instead of solely concentrating on other people's needs, projects, political issues, and pressing domestic, social, and community concerns, we begin to focus on what *we* want, on what we find personally fulfilling.

It may sound selfish, but in fact just the opposite is true. Refocusing on ourselves increases our capacity to give—making the act of giving neither altruistic nor martyrlike but rather an authentic expression of what we really care about and who we really are.

AFFIRMATION: I will give when what needs to be done matches what I genuinely want to do.

*A split second of denial. Like when you find out you're
pregnant. Of inevitability. Finality.*
—MARIGOLD FINE

If you remember back to being pregnant, you may recall a
split second in which you realized that everything had irrevo-
cably changed. You may have called the doctor back. Or run
out and bought a third EPT test, certain it just couldn't have
turned pink!

We experience a similar sense of amazement as it dawns
on us that we are actually in menopause. We may feel denial
("Not me! Not yet!"). We may hesitate to call our doctor
or tell our mother, sure it will go away if we just keep it to
ourselves.

But it won't go away. However, whereas pregnancy is
instant, menopause is a gentler, more gradual process. We
get used to the idea a little at a time, until we are able to say:

AFFIRMATION: This is really happening to me.

MONTH FOUR   **DAY TWO**

There is nothing more liberating than age.
—LIZ CARPENTER

What is it about getting older that liberates us to take more risks, to be more honest, less self-conscious and self-censoring, more willing to put ourselves on the line?

Perhaps it's that the older we are, the less we have to lose. Whether it's expressing our opinion, working for a cause, or dyeing our hair some outrageous color, we simply don't care so much what other people think. Perhaps we've learned and continue to learn how little it matters how we're judged. Or perhaps, as time goes by, we realize how precious and fleeting life is, which liberates us to live each day more authentically.

AFFIRMATION: It's liberating to grow older.

MONTH FOUR   **DAY THREE**

In my friend, I find a second self.

—ISABEL NORTON

We always need good friends to comfort and support us. To share what we're going through. To lend a helping hand, a shoulder to cry on; to give us feedback, especially right now when we're a little shaky and not so sure of ourselves.

That's why friends—or at least one very dear friend—is an irreplaceable treasure during menopause and midlife. Take a moment now to count the dearest, most intimate people in your life. Whom can you turn to when you really need a friend?

AFFIRMATION: I can always count on . . .

SELF-NURTURING

*When men reach their sixties and retire, they go to
pieces. Women go right on cooking.*

—Gail Sheehy

Gail seems to be alluding to men cracking up in midlife,
whereas women pick themselves up and do whatever's called
for.

However, cooking needn't be a chore, but rather another
way to express our creativity. If we've spent years cooking
for our family (with little or no appreciation), now we can
approach culinary tasks with a new attitude. Cooking *just* for
ourselves. Just because it feels good to throw ourselves into
baking a blueberry pie or trying out a new recipe for salmon.
Cooking needn't be a thankless, underrated job. On the
contrary it's a great way to nurture *and* nourish ourselves.

AFFIRMATION: Tonight I'll make . . .

In a dream, you are never eighty.

—ANNE SEXTON

In our dreams we often appear as a younger, more vital version of our present self.

Such reveries reflect our yearning for a time past, a time of greater sweetness and innocence, one filled with hope, promise, and possibility.

In contrast, dreams in which we appear as our current selves carry with them a sense of urgency; it's our unconscious attempt to resolve the stresses of our everyday lives. Yet we may also dream of ourselves in the future, as women of fifty, sixty, seventy, or eighty, dreams in which we catch a glimpse of what the future holds and of faraway places yet to be realized.

Try to conjure up an image of yourself as an older woman. What do you see?

AFFIRMATION: When I look into the future I see . . .

HOT FLASH: Keep a dream journal.
—ALEXANDRA W.

"Shortly after my periods stopped, I started hav-ing the most fantastic, Technicolor dreams," says Alexandra, who, at fifty-one, decided to keep a journal in which she recorded her dreams each morning upon awakening. "In one," she recalls, "I was a five-year-old, clinging to my mother's hand the first day of kindergarten. In another I dreamed I was swimming in a sea of blood."

Our dreams tell us so much. Especially in times of transition, they're worthy of our atten-tion.

What recent, vivid dreams can you recall? Some may include specific details and images. Others may simply evoke a sense or feeling that lingered after you woke up.

On the next few lines write down all you can recall of a dream you've had in the past few weeks, doing your best to remember the feelings you had following it:

I dreamed that _____

_____

_____

TRANSFORMATION

Perhaps middle age should be a period of shedding shells
—shells of ambition, material acquisition, power, shells
of the ego.

                                  —ANNE MORROW LINDBERGH

Anne Morrow Lindbergh, author of the classic memoir *Gift
from the Sea*, has so much to say in this single quotation, it's
worth devoting three days' meditations to it, one for each
"shell" she describes shedding as we go through midlife.

First the shell of ambition. Each of us reconciles our drive
and desire for career and worldly recognition in our own
way. Some of us reckon with workaholism, and commit
ourselves to a more balanced, less stressful lifestyle. Some of
us seize opportunities we've allowed to slip by, finally acting
on our unrealized dreams. Whether we slow down, speed
up, or simply take stock, we shed the external definitions of
success, replacing them with our own personal measure of
fulfillment.

**AFFIRMATION: I determine what it means to be suc-
cessful.**

MONTH FOUR   DAY NINE

. . . a time of shedding material acquisition . . .
                                        —ANNE MORROW LINDBERGH

And during midlife we begin to appreciate all we have. We
redefine the value of material things as we take pleasure in
our well-earned comforts and refine our understanding of
what's necessary and what constitutes luxuries we can live
without.

Our gratitude for what we have is tempered by an acceptance of what is beyond reach, as well as compassion for
those who have far less. Material things, however beautiful
and precious, take their rightful place in the hierarchy of
what it means to lead a rich and abundant life.

**AFFIRMATION: I determine what it means to be suc-
cessful.**

EGO

. . . and the shedding of our ego . . .
—Anne Morrow Lindbergh

And we shed the need to prove ourselves, to compete and compare, to gain love and approval by asserting our power in our relationships, in the workplace, in every sphere of life.

Shedding our ego is an ongoing spiritual process. As each year passes, our ego becomes less demanding; our need to be grandiose, to put on a facade, lessens and lessens as we feel more at ease with who we are: an utterly fallible, lovable human being.

AFFIRMATION: Slowly I shed my ego.

And we shed so many other layers of ourselves as we become closer to our own core.

—ELLEN SUE STERN

And so a fourth and final entry devoted to the concept of shedding the skins of past selves as we get closer and closer to the center of who we truly are.

We begin to let go of other things as well. We may relinquish our perfectionism, the inner pressure we create in order to live up to impossible expectations. We may shed old habits, once a necessary part of our defense and survival systems. We may give up work that is no longer fulfilling or relationships that no longer feed our hearts.

Each of us sheds different parts of ourselves, drawing nearer to our core as we come to know what's truly important in our lives.

AFFIRMATION: I'm getting closer to my essence.

> *I don't intend to age gracefully, I plan to fight it,*
> *kicking and screaming all the way.*
> —OIL OF OLAY COMMERCIAL

When I see this commercial, I assume that *graceful* is a euphemism for "giving up," for passively letting nature take its toll without putting up a fight.

But we can age gracefully without giving up. And we can fight without financing a newer, younger face. Aging gracefully simply means accepting reality and embracing change. Fighting, for some women, means lathering our face with expensive potions, perhaps even opting for a chemical peel or more extreme cosmetic surgery. For others it means an aggressive diet-and-exercise plan.

Each of us must decide for ourselves how far we're willing to go. Ultimately what matters is to put our best energy into our own self-care.

AFFIRMATION: I will age gracefully with both acceptance and assertiveness on my own behalf.

HOT FLASH: I had a face-lift and I'd do it
again in a heartbeat.

—VICKY G.

Many women are vehemently opposed to cosmetic surgery, while others, such as Vicky,
gladly go under the knife in an effort to reverse
the physical effects of aging.

Consider Molly, forty-eight, who had her "eyes
done" and says, "I always insisted I'd never do it,
but the bags under my eyes started to bother me
so much, they were all I could see when I looked
in the mirror."

Molly was pleased with the results and says
she has no regrets. This is a serious, emotionally
challenging, and expensive proposition, one
that's best left up to each of us individually, without any criticism or judgment from anyone else.

How do *you* feel about chemical peels, collagen treatments, cosmetic surgery, and other "antiaging" strategies? Do you have strong opinions, pro or con? Is your mind set, or are you still debating the possibilities? Do you have any biases one way or the other on this fairly controversial topic?

   Now's your chance to examine your attitudes. Complete this sentence:

   I feel_____

about cosmetic surgery and other techniques to reduce or camouflage aging.

—

Menopause is like going through adolescence a second time.

—HENRIETTA BENSUSSEN

Yes and no. The shifting hormones, physical discomforts, mood swings, and identity crises are reminiscent of adolescence.

As grown women we experience a similar roller coaster; however, the ride is smoother because we are more prepared to cope. We have confidence that we will find ways of enduring the challenges. We have patience that it will ease up in time. We have perspective, which keeps us from overreacting. And we have a well-earned sense of self that keeps us rooted and strong, able to navigate through this tumultuous time.

AFFIRMATION: I am older now and more capable of handling this hormonal shift.

TRANSFORMATION

Is the fully opened rose not as beautiful as the bud?
—JANE MICKELSON

Hardly! Imagine a ripe rose, its petals stretching outward, its deep rich hue a metaphor for the rare beauty of women in midlife.

There is grace and beauty in every stage of our maturation. The adolescent girl in her budding sensuality reminds us of life's possibility. The young woman in her vibrant, ripening self makes us stare in appreciation.

But the fully grown woman, a breathtaking flower in full bloom, gives us a glimpse of what it means to be open, all the way there.

AFFIRMATION: My beauty is growing on me.

MONTH FOUR   **DAY SEVENTEEN**

In youth we learn, in age we understand.
                    —MARIA VON EBNER-ESCHENBACH

Of course we never understand everything. If we did, we'd have nothing left to live for.

But greater understanding is one of the gifts gained as we travel life's path. We know more today than we did yesterday. We look back with clarity, insight, and perspective. It's not that we stop learning. On the contrary, we are better students than ever. We apply new concepts, interpret our experiences, and integrate what we know with what we're newly discovering each day.

AFFIRMATION: I "get" the lessons in a new and deeper way.

TIME

The longer we live, the more time we have to pursue the things that make life meaningful.
—MARIANNE WILLIAMSON

Depending on our age and circumstances, we may have more or less time to do all the things we've dreamed of but haven't gotten around to. Those of us coping with growing children and aging parents as well as marriage, career, and other involvements may find our schedules more stressed than ever. If, on the other hand, our children are grown, our careers are less demanding, our income more stable, we may indeed enjoy the luxury of more time to ourselves.

In either case, as we get older, time seems to pass more quickly. Valuing ourselves means valuing our time—making sure we spend it in ways that enhance the quality of our lives.

AFFIRMATION: I will use my time well.

Sleep deprivation can be used to torture prisoners. It was driving me crazy!

—EVELYN M. PARKER

Insomnia: "Slumber broken by restless (and often damp) interruptions." Walking around in a daze, crabby, headachy and out of sorts are some of the not-so-good parts of menopause for some women.

This is worth talking about for two reasons: (a) so that we don't feel crazy when we're actually exhausted; and (b) so that we can come up with some strategies for living with sleep deprivation.

Here are what some very tired women recommend:

- Build in naps
- Cut back your schedule
- Meditate daily
- Eat regular, healthy meals

Above all else, don't feel guilty or let anyone give you a hard time. Rest is required for functioning. Do *whatever* you can to make up for lost sleep.

AFFIRMATION: You'd be crabby too!

HOT FLASH: Try Women's Tonic Tea.
—PELA SANDER

This and other exotic, herbal remedies for fatigue and other menopause symptoms are included in Sander's informative essay from *Women of the Fourteenth Moon*.

Here's the recipe:

1 part red raspberry leaf
1 part nettle leaf
1 part motherwort
1/4 to 1/2 part fennel seed

Pela Sander also recommends a balanced diet consisting of 40 to 60 percent whole grains; 10 to 20 percent organic vegetables and fruits; 10 to 15 percent dairy, eggs, and meat; and 5 percent seaweed.

Sounds like a trip to the health food store is in order, a worthwhile effort if it helps ease discomfort and makes us feel good.

Just about every woman I interviewed for this book mentioned diet as one of the best weapons against hot flashes, sleep deprivation, osteoporosis, and other menopausal issues.

Several mentioned vitamin supplements, especially vitamin E. Now it's time to assess your nutritional plan. Write down everything you eat and drink during a typical day in your life:

Breakfast:_____
Lunch:_____
Dinner:_____
Snacks:_____

Now determine whether you're doing your best to nourish yourself right now.

No more tampons or pads. No more cramps. No more premenstrual stress. Freedom!

—EVELYN PARKER

Now for some very tangible benefits most menopausal women celebrate.

It is liberating, not to mention money-saving, to no longer stock tampons, sanitary pads, and all the other menstrual-period paraphernalia. Especially women for whom PMS has been a monthly crisis—energy sapping and emotionally draining—menopause can be a welcome change, worthy of saying:

AFFIRMATION: Thank God I don't have my period. Period.

Month Four   **Day Twenty-three**

Knowing these cycles are short-lived suddenly makes them precious.

—Marigold Fine

On the other hand, like so many things in life, what we've taken for granted suddenly takes on value as we consider the possibility of its loss.

Most of us certainly took our periods for granted (there were, after all, some four hundred and eight cycles, give or take a few). Except for times of pregnancy, we simply assumed every twenty-eight or thirty days we'd be "visited" by a flow we'd come to expect, accept, and live with.

Now our periods are bittersweet. Knowing they will become lighter, less frequent, and ultimately taper off makes us more aware that we are changing, that what is here today will not necessarily be here tomorrow.

AFFIRMATION: Everything in life is fleeting and precious.

One day I said to myself, "I'm forty!" By the time I'd recovered from the shock of that discovery, I had reached fifty.

—SIMONE DE BEAUVOIR

It takes a while to sink in. Sometimes we have a delayed reaction; sometimes we're shocked into awareness. A friend's fortieth-birthday invitation startles us into recognition that ours is on the way. Our son's wedding, the birth of our first grandchild, a co-worker's retirement forces us to stop in our tracks, look honestly at ourselves and say, "I'm forty," "I'm fifty," "I'm sixty."

Slowly we catch up with our mirror's reflection. Slowly we grow into our new selves until being forty or fifty or sixty seems like the most natural thing in the world.

AFFIRMATION: I will take the time I need to discover who I have become.

Menopause? I don't remember it at all.
> —MY MOTHER (AND LOTS OF OTHER MOTHERS)

What *is* it about our mothers that they can't remember their
first period, they can't recall what labor felt like, and now,
when we turn to them for counsel, they can't remember
going through menopause?

Over and over again women report that their mothers
describe menopause as a nonevent; they are either surprised
or dismissive when we try to explain the intense changes we
are experiencing.

Perhaps it's simply that our mothers had neither the language nor the support needed to name and affirm their experience of menopause.

But we do! And if we can't do it with our mothers, then
let's do it with our sisters and friends. So that someday,
when our daughters turn to *us* and say, "Mom, tell me about
your menopause," we can say:

AFFIRMATION: Honey, here's how it was for me.

PAMPERING

I, for one, plan to work out exactly what I've invested in "feminine hygiene products" for 36 plus years—and make an equal contribution to pampering myself.
—Elayne Clift

Great idea!

A quick estimate of money spent on menstrual-related products since the age of thirteen comes out to a pretty hefty sum.

What if we were to spend even a tenth of that pampering ourselves as a tangible reward for entering menopause? How about a week at a spa? A beautiful new hat? Our favorite gourmet coffee? A pint of fresh raspberries? The sexy black camisole we spotted in a catalog?

How much to spend is immaterial. What matters is to give yourself a treat that symbolizes the money you're saving.

AFFIRMATION: I'm worth it.

HOT FLASH: Pamper yourself!

—ANNA R.

If there's one thing women in midlife repeatedly recommend, it's to make the time and spend the money—however modest—to pamper ourselves.

For Anna, a forty-seven-year-old minister, this meant giving herself one day off a month and devote it to reading in bed. (Which was no small feat, considering her grueling schedule!)

Some women browse in bookstores, get a facial, or take off for a weekend in the woods as a way of giving themselves a treat.

Perhaps as we age, we're finally realizing that we count. That it's not only permissible but advisable to treat ourselves right!

Prepare to pamper yourself!

This is an order! One foolproof Rx for the ups and downs of menopause is an occasional treat —preferably on a regular basis.

What are *you* willing to do to pamper yourself? Make one promise right now.

Here's how I plan to pamper myself:

A clear statement of a patriarchal attitude: When a woman can no longer bear children, she is no longer of use.

—ANN MANKOWITZ

Motherhood may or may not have been one way in which we've gained fulfillment. But it's only part of what makes us whole.

Today we recognize and celebrate diverse choices. We can be mothers, wives, single, child-free, executives, astronauts, community volunteers, or anything and everything in between.

As we enter midlife, whether or not motherhood has been a primary source of self-esteem, we find new ways of expressing ourselves, discovering myriad ways to be of use.

AFFIRMATION: I am a mother and much, much more.

> *There's a time when everything comes good for you—*
> *your humor. Your style. Your bad temper.*
>
> —GERMAINE GREER

Spend some time with women in their fifties and sixties—you'll notice there's lots of laughter, giggling, and cackling. We no longer take ourselves so seriously; we've lightened up and are able to laugh at ourselves.

Look closely at a group of older women and notice their apparel. Each is distinctive. One throws a red wool scarf over her shoulder. Another is a vision in lace. Still another sports jeans, boots, and a big sweater, her signature style.

And then there's the bad temper. Notice also our willingness to get mad. To speak our minds, to scream out against injustice, or just to be curmudgeons—yet another midlife benefit to celebrate.

AFFIRMATION: There's no need to censor myself anymore.

In Native American tradition you only become fully grown at fifty-one.

—ERICA LANN CLARK

Here's another enlightening culturally different way to look at midlife.

What *does* it mean to be fully grown up? It means that we know and celebrate who we are. It means we trust ourselves and make clear choices based on experience and wisdom. It means we don't answer to anyone or in any way diminish or qualify ourselves. It means we are active agents in our own destiny, fully responsible for our past, our present, and who we are becoming in the future.

AFFIRMATION: It's great to be all grown up.

Beware of any article, book or person who tries to convince you that menopause is an illness.

—JANE MICKELSON

Here's another apt analogy to pregnancy. I can't count the times I've counseled expectant mothers to think of pregnancy as a natural, healthy state and *not* an illness.

The same applies here. But with one caveat: While neither pregnancy nor menopause is a sickness, they *are* both physiological conditions requiring at least a modicum of medical care.

On the one hand we don't want to be treated—or to treat ourselves—as invalids. On the other hand we must be sure to take our symptoms seriously, with an ongoing commitment to getting the best possible medical care.

AFFIRMATION: If I am feeling under the weather, it's okay to say so.

There was a time when the ads said, "Wash away the ugly gray."

—MAXINE HONG KINGSTON

Some still do. In researching this book I came across at least half a dozen hair-care commercials and a fair amount of magazine ads that still capitalize on people's viewing aging as ugly in order to sell products.

It's a shame. And it's a powerful message that deeply affects how we see our own gray hair and what we choose to do or not do about it.

Here's one way to combat a negative media image. Instead of "washing it away," what if every woman wore her gray hair as a crown, proudly announcing to the world:

AFFIRMATION: Here I am in all my glory.

I love Premarin. It's my candidate for the greatest discovery in all history.

—CANDIDA LAWRENCE

Here's another in a series of contradictory reviews of hormone replacement therapy that hopefully offer a balanced, unbiased look at the pros and cons.

Some women swear by estrogen, progestin, and Premarin (not necessarily all of the above), even going so far as to throw fits in their doctors' offices until they're clutching a prescription in their hands.

Other women want nothing to do with HRT and are absolutely committed to alternative remedies for hot flashes and other symptoms.

Most women fall somewhere in between. Throughout this book take in the vast range of opinions on this debate. Measure them against your personal experience, with an open, receptive mind.

AFFIRMATION: I will educate myself on the pros and cons of HRT.

Hormones slap you up against the door of your unfinished business.

—MAURA KELSEY

Times of intense emotional and physical changes are often the best opportunities for personal growth.

As we struggle with internal hormonal rages, we may finally face a lifetime of poor eating habits, addictive behavior, the fact that we've neglected our health, or the need to improve our relationships. We're hit with the realization that it's time to confront our lives honestly.

Areas of unresolved anger and pain are "up" for healing, if we're willing to make the effort. It may not feel like an opportunity—healing is hard work—but the payoffs are huge!

AFFIRMATION: Now's as good a time as any to face unfinished business in my life.

HOT FLASH: Resolve your relationship
with your parents.

—PATRICIA W.

"If you're lucky enough to still have your parents
in your life, make a commitment to heal any unresolved conflicts with them," advises Patricia,
age fifty, who did just that with her aging parents.

Midlife offers a rare opportunity to confront unfinished business, heal old pain, and make
peace with ourselves in the present. Some
women begin counseling, some attend seminars, some join a support group, and others simply work on their issues by focusing on areas
creating or contributing to emotional distress.

Anything—and I repeat: *anything*—we do to
enhance our mental health is a step in the right
direction.

What unhealed pain, unresolved conflicts, and unfinished business remain in your life, keeping you from finding happiness and peace?

Each of us has her own unique cutting edges—the areas of our lives that need work. What are yours? What are you willing to do about it? As honestly as you can, answer the following questions:

I'm aware that I need to work on . . .

I'm willing to . . .

MEDIA IMAGES

> *Women in the movies never go to the bathroom, have*
> *periods or cramps, let alone hot flashes and night sweats.*
> —PAT RHODA

Try to come up with one—just one—example of a television or movie star for whom menopause was a visible part of her character.

I couldn't come up with one, which is one reason why we feel so isolated, when in fact some estimated forty or fifty million women will enter midlife in the year 2000.

Although neither TV nor movies depict real life, they mirror reality and create our perceptions, positive and negative. So here's my suggestion for a pilot: A fifty-year-old-woman, maybe Marlo Thomas, struggles to keep her marriage alive, her career booming, her self-esteem high in the midst of menopause. Call it *That Woman!*

AFFIRMATION: What about *Fortysomething?* And *Fiftysomething* next season?

Age is something that doesn't matter unless you're a cheese.

—BILLIE BURKE

It *does* matter! And all the ''You're in the prime of your life'' greeting-card sentiments don't mean a thing when we look in the mirror and begin to come to terms with the reality that time is in fact taking its toll.

Which isn't to discourage us from cultivating a positive attitude toward the wonderful aspects of midlife. Optimism is okay—so long as it doesn't require us to deny our sadness and grief. They, too, are a real and necessary part of accepting who we are and where we are.

AFFIRMATION: It matters.

It took twelve years from the first hot flash to the last drop of blood.

—MARJORIE NELSON

A common myth of menopause is that it is a single event rather than a gradual process during which time our menses slowly come to a stop.

The actual symptoms of menopause may come on suddenly; our first missed period or first hot flash may feel like a sudden and singular event. But in reality menopause happens over time. Which fortunately gives us time, be it five years, ten years, or longer, to adapt slowly to the change.

AFFIRMATION: I have time.

MONTH FIVE   **DAY ELEVEN**

Before, I was a together woman! Then, menopause. I felt like a split atom, no longer in control.
—CLARA E. WOOD

The sensation of going to pieces, of being utterly out of control, is expressed repeatedly by women in menopause.

It's scary to feel as if our lives are in chaos. And to a certain degree they are! Hormonal changes are happening to us, regardless of what we do or don't do. Our periods diminish or stop entirely whether or not we're ready.

It's hard to feel as if we're falling apart. But it's only temporary. With time, patience, and a little extra room to feel a little crazy, we will reintegrate our new selves into a whole, cohesive being, more "together" than ever.

AFFIRMATION: I am not going to pieces.

COPING WITH HOT FLASHES

When the hot flashes came, she'd sit down in the closest chair, move her hands like fans about her face. "Here it comes again. This is hell."

—PATRICE VECCHIONE

In this essay from *Women of the Fourteenth Moon,* Patricia Vecchione describes her memories of her mother's menopause, saying, "She'd call out to God, 'Why are you doing this to me?' She'd reach for a tissue, take off her glasses, and mop her face. She'd hold my hand tightly through the heat wave, sweat beading on her forehead."

Colorful descriptions of hot flashes abound; "I wake up three or four times a night, soaked to the bone, dripping wet, with sweat running down my legs," says one woman. Another says, "It's my own personal summer; it can be freezing cold, but I'm so steamy, it may as well be ninety degrees in the shade."

However we describe them, those of us for whom hot flashes are a reality can attest to their powerful—and often disturbing—effect in our lives. Like labor contractions, each one causes us to stop, breathe, and wait until it's over.

AFFIRMATION: It will pass.

HOT FLASH: Always carry a fan.

—JILL A.

It's the simplest, easiest, most traditional way women have—and continue—to deal with hot flashes. In fact some groups of menopausal women humorously refer to themselves as the Fan Club—an apt name if there ever was one.

According to Jill, age fifty-six, who suffers from constant hot flashes, "Carrying a fan isn't only helpful, it's also a terrific creative release." Since entering menopause, Jill has begun collecting a vast array of beautiful fans, some paper, some silk, which she has proudly displayed on her dining-room mantel.

I can't think of a better symbol for the beauty of women in midlife.

Finding ways to counter the effects of hot flashes is a primary concern for most menopausal women. Here are some creative tips from other women:

- Keep a cooler filled with ice next to your bed
- Carry a squirt bottle
- Wear layers

Can you add more ideas to the list?

MONTH FIVE   **DAY FIFTEEN**

The most creative force in the world is the menopausal woman with zest.

—MARGARET MEAD

Here's the flip side: Being reproduction-free opens up a wellspring of creative energy. Women in midlife are on fire! (excuse the pun), fairly exploding with originality and the drive to see our ideas through.

Creativity expands as we throw ourselves full-force into life and all it has to offer. Zest indeed! What a perfect adjective for the renewed excitement with which we face each day.

AFFIRMATION: I am experiencing a rebirth in creativity.

SUPPORT

I have been measured, tested, bled, scanned, rayed, wired, picked, poked, advised and prescribed.
—GAYLE SAND

So says Gayle Sand in her best-seller *Is It Hot in Here or Is It Me?*, which describes her endless and exhausting search for medical relief for her midlife symptoms.

Many of us know just what she's talking about. The search for information, advice, and remedies may take more out of us than menopause itself. Waiting in doctors' offices, undergoing painful examinations, bone-density measurements, trying to get a handle on the Great Hormone Debate, takes time and money and saps our energy. Which is why it's so vitally important to choose a supportive medical provider you like, trust, and feel absolutely comfortable with.

AFFIRMATION: Sometimes I feel like a human guinea pig.

*So I took off my high heels (they hurt my feet), let my
hair go gray and replaced sex with food.*
                                        —ERICA LANN CLARK

Freedom of choice is the operative principle here. In midlife
we become less malleable, more true to ourselves, freer to
be deliberate in our choices.

And *all* the choices are open to us. We can wear high
heels or high-tops, let our hair go gray, get foils, or find out
whether blondes really do have more fun. We can have sex
instead of food, food instead of sex, or have them together,
eating ice cream out of the carton in bed after making love.
The point is: *We get to choose.* No one decides what is right
for us.

AFFIRMATION: I have the freedom to choose.

*If I ever write my autobiography it will be called, "I
hate you, Doris Day!"*

—INA LEA MEIBACH

We each have our own version of Doris Day—that fifties
media creation and caricature of the "perfect woman," who
exemplified all the qualities of niceness, compliance, passivity, and domestic fulfillment.

Donna Reed was my personal nemesis; my children still
tease me by calling me Madonna Reed, their loving way of
reassuring me it's okay not to have fresh-baked cookies when
they get home from school.

But humor aside, these images were damaging and limit-
ing; we may still feel guilt-ridden when we fall short of
cultural expectations, when we don't fit the social norm.

And in midlife we can stop reacting against these images
that subtly or blatantly keep us from loving and accepting
who we are, knowing that, for whatever it's worth:

**AFFIRMATION: Doris and Donna weren't as happy as
they looked.**

It is never too late to be what you might have been.
—GEORGE ELIOT

These inspiring words remind us that there's still time to do the things we've dreamed of but haven't gotten around to for lack of confidence, resources, or because the timing just wasn't right.

At forty-one my friend Jan went back to school to get a graduate degree in education. At forty-four my friend Susan started her own, now-very-successful line of children's apparel. At fifty my friend George learned to play the violin.

Now, in midlife, the time is ripe to take our dreams off the back burner and find out what's possible if we're willing to give life our best shot.

AFFIRMATION: Nothing ventured, nothing gained.

HOT FLASH: Just do it!

—NIKE AD

If you've always wanted to water-ski, why wait a moment longer? If you've fantasized playing the saxophone, call your local music store and sign up for lessons. If you've been talking about quitting your secure-but-not-particularly-challenging job in order to start your own business, make today the day you stop talking and start doing something to make your dreams come through.

As the Nike ad says—and lots of midlife women who have taken the plunge agree—just do it and you'll most likely wonder what took you so long to create the kind of life you've dreamed of.

What risks are you ready to take in order to fulfill your dreams? It needn't be something dramatic, just choose one new hobby, vocation, or adventure you're willing to embark on right now. In the following space write down the one life-changing step you're ready to take:

In the next six months I commit to:

SELF-CONFIDENCE

Now I feel less and less that I have anything to prove.
                                        —KAY PRESTON

What a great leap of self-confidence to no longer feel the need to prove anything, least of all to ourselves. We no longer have to knock ourselves out dazzling friends with gourmet dinners, getting dressed up to make an impression, fighting to be at the top of our class or our company as a way of proving our worth.

For so long we've had to push ourselves in order to convince ourselves—and others—that we're, as the character "Stuart Smalley" says, "good enough, smart enough, and, doggone it, people *like* us." We are gradually coming to know—really know—that:

AFFIRMATION: I have absolutely nothing to prove.

> *Now that I couldn't have children, maybe he'd want*
> *some high-heeled, mini-skirted, nubile young thing with*
> *enough eggs to populate a major city.*
>
> —GAYLE SAND

It's that "younger woman" fear again. We worry that our mate may be attracted to some "sexy young thing" in his aerobics class. In some dark corner in the back of our minds, we torment ourselves with fantasies fueled by real-life horror stories of "home wreckers" on the loose.

The physical effects of aging mixed with the emotionally sobering realization that we can no longer reproduce can easily make us feel threatened and insecure. Which is why it's important right now to rekindle romance with our mate. And why it's important to cultivate shared interests, dreams, and goals. And most of all why we need to seek reassurance that we're still the love of his life.

AFFIRMATION: I'm irreplaceable.

MORTALITY

That slightly sagging chin was fate serving notice.
> —MAGGIE SCARF

Which is one reason why the physical changes of midlife are so scary and upsetting.

The lines on our faces are artifacts of time passed, evidence that we are getting older, like it or not. The streaks of silver and gray, the bags under our eyes, the creases in our once-smooth palm herald our mortality, with stunning, irrevocable clarity.

But here's the irony: *How* we respond to fate's notice affects how we look. If we're embarrassed and resentful of our aging, it shows. If, however, we accept and welcome our mortality with grace, our appearance takes on a glow and a beauty that only comes with time.

AFFIRMATION: I can fight fate or I can welcome what comes with confidence.

We're young, we're old, we're neither, we're both. Each age has a beautiful gift, its own brand of joy and sorrow.

—MARIANNE WILLIAMSON

Can you remember your anxiety as a teenager? The zit-fits? Clothes crises? Fat attacks?

We tend to romanticize our youth, our high-school years, our early twenties as a time when we felt pretty, confident, ready to take on the world. In fact those times, just like these times, contained their fair share of grief. And a good measure of happiness. Just as this stage contains some of each.

Take a moment right now to think about the inherent gifts present in midlife:

AFFIRMATION: I am aware of the gift of . . .

MONTH FIVE   **DAY TWENTY-SIX**

*Two-thirds of American women say nothing to anybody
as they approach menopause.*

—GAIL SHEEHY

What a discouraging comment on how isolated we feel.

My own recent overtures on this subject met with disbelief, subtle reproaches, and a general attitude of "Give me a break! Why are you thinking about *that?*" My husband shuddered, my mother laughed, even my gynecologist brushed me off, seemingly peeved that I'd brought up the topic.

But my fortieth birthday is right around the bend. My cycles are shortening, my migraines are worsening; this seems as good a time as any to start exploring the early stages of menopause.

When we're dismissed, we shut up and stop sharing. That's the worst thing we can do to ourselves. Let's hope that by the year 2000, women will naturally, easily turn to one another and say:

AFFIRMATION: Let's talk about menopause.

HOT FLASH: Tell your husband and children what's going on.

—DEBORAH K.

"The worst mistake I made was to try to keep my menopause a secret," says Deborah, age fifty-two. "My husband, my children, even my friends thought I was acting incredibly weird, and they had no idea why. When I finally told them, they couldn't have been more supportive."

Candor is key to getting understanding and support as we struggle with mood swings, medications, hot flashes, and all the other aspects of menopause. There's no need to suffer in silence. *Express* your feelings. *Educate* your family and friends. *Embrace* all the love that's there for you if you're willing to be real.

Support is essential right now. Being able to share your feelings will help you cope with the emotional ups and downs.

Take a moment now to consider your circle of support. Whom can you talk to? Whine to? Whom do you ask for advice? To whom do you confide your most intimate feelings and thoughts?

List all the people you count on for support:

1. _____
2. _____
3. _____

Now, in your own way, acknowledge your gratitude.

Over the next two decades forty or fifty million women
will pass through the Change.
—NATIONAL BUREAU OF STATISTICS

We're reaching a critical mass. We have literally millions of
other women with whom to learn about menopause, lobby
for medical advances, and join in a collective effort to give
midlife the respect it deserves as a profound and transforma-
tive life passage.

And we have our work cut out for us. Some of us will
become politically active in this decade. Some of us will
form or join support groups with other midlife women. And
others will simply turn to one other woman and say:

AFFIRMATION: Hi. I'm_____**. I'm in menopause.**

Is this what's next? At my age? But I'm a kid!
—CANDICE BERGEN

Last year we watched as her character, "Murphy Brown," became a single mother, setting off sparks all the way to the White House, provoking criticism from then–vice president Dan Quayle, who apparently had trouble separating fantasy from reality.

Perhaps next year's series will focus on this "middle-aged" new mom beginning to contemplate her transition to midlife before millions of viewers.

I hope so. The more vibrant, gorgeous forty- and fifty-year-old women we see, the better we feel about ourselves.

AFFIRMATION: I'm starting to see midlife in a whole new light.

MONTH SIX **DAY ONE**

The Japanese language doesn't even have a word for hot flashes.

—ANONYMOUS

Does this mean that Japanese women don't experience hot flashes and therefore don't need a vocabulary with which to describe them?

Maybe so. The fact that the English language *does* include the term *hot flashes* gives us a way of talking about what we're feeling. Think about how hard it would be to explain to your mate or your doctor: "I had this weird thing happen last night. Prickly heat streamed down my body, and wet sweat drenched through my nightgown."

Saying, "I had a hot flash," or "hot flush" as some women call them, is a valuable code word, if you will, that we easily, quickly understand.

AFFIRMATION: I'm glad we have a way to talk about this.

REMORSE

*Earlier I was struggling with my life. I shouldn't have
had children.*

—Deena Metzger

Midlife is a time of reckoning. In retrospect we can see:
"Looking back, I realize I was too immature to go away to
college" or "not really ready for marriage" or "too confused to have chosen the career I did at the time."

These revelations can be valuable in that they shed light on
our past decisions and how they turned out. Honest evalua-
tion of mistakes is useful as long as we don't get stuck in
guilt and remorse. The trick is to apply our newfound insight to our present lives so that we don't repeat the past.

AFFIRMATION: Now I know myself better.

MONTH SIX   **DAY THREE**

*He's talking about my insides like he's some kind of
building inspector.*

—GAYLE SAND

Dry vaginal walls. Decreased secretions. Pretty cold, impersonal
language for the emotionally charged experience of menopause.

We can't rewrite the Menopause Dictionary, although female poets and essayists are doing their best to convey the
richness of our experience. What we *can* do is find a medical
provider who speaks to us personally, sensitively, using language that helps us understand what we're going through.

AFFIRMATION: This is my body we're talking about!

INCONTINENCE

*Now it's a caution not to laugh too hard or stray too
far from a restroom.*

—Gretchen Sentchen

Incontinence is the topic, whether it's an occasional trickle
or a constant flow—all-too-common side effects of menopause affecting lots of women and causing a fair share of
embarrassment.

Frankly I thought twice before including this subject, then
quickly realized incontinence was one more taboo, easily
shied away from and thus making it that much more important to address.

Like any physical symptom, coping requires strategies:
pantiliners or Depends, watching liquid intake, regular bath-
room visits, and in more extreme cases medication prescribed by your health care provider.

And like any other issue, it requires empathy and understanding. If you're one of the thousands of women trying not
to laugh, know that:

**AFFIRMATION: You're not alone. And there's nothing
to be embarrassed about.**

This new identity is not one I grow into easily.
—CONNIE BATTEN

We look in the mirror, surprised by the fine lines that appear around our eyes. We look at our adolescent daughters, shocked that they're big enough to borrow our clothes. We look at the clock by our bedside, chagrined to see that it's only nine o'clock and we're ready to turn in for the night.

Have we turned into someone else? Has the "old familiar me" disappeared forever?

Yes and no. As we age, we shed certain aspects of our old selves, yet we continue to carry the experiences that have shaped us. We are both old *and* new, who we were as well as who we are becoming, which is exciting, scary, and a necessary part of growth.

AFFIRMATION: I'm still the old me, only better.

HOT FLASH: Notice all the ways you're getting better.

—Dana S.

Dana, a high-school English teacher who recently celebrated her fiftieth birthday, counts patience, tolerance, and increased stamina among the qualities she's acquired over the past few years. She says, "Focusing on the positives helps counter the negative aspects of menopause."

It's sound advice. Most of us improve with age. We get smarter. Healthier. More responsible. More skilled at what we do. As Mary Jane, an interior designer in her late forties, says, "Ten years ago I was competent at my career. Today I consider myself a master."

There's nothing conceited about acknowledging our growth. It's another way of celebrating getting older.

In what ways are *you* getting better as you grow older? It's time to take inventory. What skills, qualities, and abilities are you acquiring as you mature?

Complete this sentence as many times as you can:

I'm proud to say that now I can . . .

MONTH SIX   **DAY EIGHT**

Archie: Edith, if you're gonna have a change, you gotta do it right now! I'm gonna give you just thirty seconds, now c'mon, change!
          —"ARCHIE BUNKER" WRITTEN BY NORMAN LEAR

At times we may feel pressured to hurry through menopause. We get impatient with its seemingly endless discomforts, anxious about the toll it's taking on our relationships, our career, the havoc it's wreaking in our daily routines.

But there's no rushing it. This natural process takes as long as it takes. For some women it's a two-year process; others feel affected for upward of ten years.

We can't change any faster than we are changing. We can, however, change our own urgency, accepting that:

AFFIRMATION: Nature has her own pace.

I was the only self-avowed menopausal woman in my son's preschool.

—MARCIA WALKER

As we're waiting longer to conceive, the time gap between pregnancy and menopause is closing in. Many of us are mothering small children while simultaneously coping with the pressures of midlife.

As "older mothers," it's especially important to build a support system with other women in their forties who are facing similar challenges. There's no need to be isolated. There are lots of women out there just like us, going through the very same thing.

AFFIRMATION: I'll find them.

INFORMATION

I am never afraid of what I know.

—ANNA SEWELL

What's unknown is almost always scarier than the most so-bering reality. That's why it's so important to arm ourselves with credible information and up-to-date resources regarding medical aspects of menopause.

Information comes from lots of different places: from the most current medical journals, from your medical provider, from social service agencies, *and* from other women.

We must share everything we know with one another. Doing so helps diminish fear and increases our collective and individual confidence, enabling us to make better, more in-formed choices.

AFFIRMATION: The more I know, the more secure I feel.

Today's coalescents are mapping out a whole new stage of life.

—GAIL SHEEHY

Sheehy has coined the term *coalescents* to describe the coming together that occurs during midlife.

So many things begin to fall into place as we map out the next twenty or thirty years of our lives. Our values are clearer and more well defined. Our past experiences are integrated with the new discoveries we are making. Our sense of self becomes more cohesive as we slowly coalesce into the person we are becoming.

AFFIRMATION: I feel the different parts of myself coming together in a new way.

For the first time in years, I grew a garden.
—EMMA JOY CRONE

Ahh . . . the primal pleasure of digging in fresh, moist dirt, planting next spring's tomatoes, tending our perennials, grateful for their awesome, annual appearance.

At every stage of life women take part in planting, tending, and nurturing. Whether we are raising children or raising tulips, participating in nature's cycles makes us feel connected and alive.

Right now is the perfect time to cultivate a garden. To celebrate your midlife, plant one thing, even if it's an avocado seed in a glass on your windowsill. Watch it grow.

AFFIRMATION: I reaffirm my connection to nature.

HOT FLASH: Take long walks by yourself.
—TERRI M.

"I started walking a mile each morning before work, and it really helped," says Terri, age fifty-three, whose menopausal mood swings were so intense, she considered herself "certifiable."

Solitary walks are a good way of building energy and restoring emotional balance. Being outdoors, where we can look at the sky, breathe fresh air, maybe even pick a leaf or two, deepens our spirituality.

There are lots of different ways of connecting with nature. Some women swim, some jog, some simply sit beneath a tree. What matters is to let nature nurture us in any way we can.

How are you letting nature work her wonders in your life? When's the last time you went camping in the woods? Walked around the lake? Waded in the water or gazed at the stars?

Make a commitment to do at least one thing every single day that will help you feel closer and more connected to nature.

I commit to . . .

Prayer has been essential for me.
——PATRICIA MATHES CANE

There is tremendous power in prayer. Not necessarily through organized religion but rather the personal meditative moment in which we express our longings, seek guidance, and give thanks to a higher power, however we define it.

During menopause we may be especially in need of prayer: when we feel frustrated or angry; when we wonder why our body is betraying us, why our husband doesn't "get it," why we feel so lost, confused, and alone.

Then it's good to say a prayer. It's a way of saying:

AFFIRMATION: This is too big for me to handle all alone.

MONTH SIX   **DAY SIXTEEN**

*Most women will traverse the difficult transition from
reproductive animal to reflective animal during menopause.*

—GERMAINE GREER

No matter how introspective we are, our busy schedules may
have precluded being able to sit still, alone with our
thoughts, reflective and responsive to our innermost
thoughts.

Now it's important to make the time. To commit to a
regular period in which to meditate. Do it every single day.
Whether you keep a journal, practice yoga or Transcendental
Meditation, or just sit silently by yourself, make it a discipline and take it seriously.

**AFFIRMATION: I have so much to reflect upon right
now.**

Women today reaching menopause at around age fifty can expect to live twenty-five to forty more years—one third or more of their lives.

—GENIA PAULI HADDON

So how will we spend the next thirty or forty years? And what are we doing—today—in order to prepare to live them fully and fruitfully?

Is our energy winding down or increasing as we age? Are we making a concerted effort to eat well, exercise, and do everything possible to secure our health? Are we stuck in an unfulfilling vocation, or are we finding ways to constantly revitalize? Are we settling into our relationships or are we making sure to keep them alive?

What are *you* doing to make sure you're making the most of your life?

AFFIRMATION: I have so much life left to live.

UNIQUENESS

Other women seem to float through menopause.
— NANCY V.

When I conduct Expecting Change workshops, the first thing I notice is every expectant mother frantically comparing notes: What are *you* doing for morning sickness? How much weight have *you* gained? How do you feel about epidurals? Breast-feeding? Day care?

Similarly we seek feedback and confirmation from other women in menopause. It's natural to compare ourselves; it helps to hear other women's stories so long as we remember, just as in pregnancy, that each woman's menopause is as unique and individual as a snowflake. We can seek reassurance without having to be just like somebody else.

AFFIRMATION: I won't compare myself with any other woman.

*Either you give me estrogen or the next time I have a
hot flash I'm going to rip my clothes off and shout your
name.*

—"BARBARA," QUOTED BY GAIL SHEEHY

This dramatic ultimatum was one woman's way of putting
her foot down—hard—and insisting on the estrogen she was
convinced would make a critical difference in her menopause.

This isn't the only—or even the most—extreme example
I've heard from women frustrated by having to argue, convince, cajole, and even bribe their medical provider in order
to begin hormone replacement therapy.

If this applies to you, whether it's wanting HRT or not,
whether you're just tired of being patronized or kept waiting
too long for appointments, don't tolerate being treated this
way. Raise your voice! Insist on respect. And if you don't get
results, don't be afraid to walk out the door and into a better
relationship with a medical provider who gives you what you
need.

AFFIRMATION: It doesn't have to be this hard.

HOT FLASH: Shop around for the right doctor.

—SUZANNE L.

"Remember, you're the customer!" says Suzanne, who interviewed a half-dozen practitioners before she settled on a female gynecologist in whom to trust during her menopause.

It's natural to feel intimidated or overwhelmed at the thought of "shopping" for the right doctor, who, as Suzanne reminds us, "isn't necessarily the same one who delivered your babies. In fact," she adds, "I stopped seeing my OBGYN after fifteen years and two children when I noticed I was the only woman in the waiting room who wasn't pregnant."

Other women in menopause are your best referral source for finding a medical provider with whom you feel comfortable and safe.

Here is a suggested list of interview questions when you are ready to "shop" for a medical provider:

- What percentage of your practice consists of women in menopause?
- How do you feel about hormone replacement therapy?
- What is your attitude toward alternative remedies?
- What role do you believe diet plays during menopause?
- How many hysterectomies a year do you perform?
- At what age do you recommend bone-density testing?
- How long, on average, are your scheduled appointments? How long, on average, do patients wait to be seen?
- What insurance coverage do you handle?

Now add four more questions to the list.

SPIRIT

Isadora was dancing right up to the time she died.
—MAXINE HONG KINGSTON

Flamboyant Isadora Duncan left us with the colorful image of her long scarf flying in the wind.

Every day of our lives is another opportunity to renew our commitment to life and to take advantage of the fact that we're here and that it's up to us to make the most of it.

None of us know when our final moment will come. This is true whether we're eighteen or eighty. But midlife is a particularly prime time to reexamine whether we're just passing time or living up to our potential, fully alive in every cell of our being.

AFFIRMATION: I'm totally in my life.

MONTH SIX   DAY TWENTY-THREE

My dream is to reach a point when age is irrelevant.
                                                —INA LEA MEIBACH

It's a reachable dream *if* our goal is for our age to be irrelevant to *ourselves*.

We can't transform society overnight; it will take years, perhaps generations, to alter our cultural obsession with youth and intolerance toward aging.

Others may always see our age as significant, each birthday symbolizing new limits to what we are capable of.

How we see ourselves, on the other hand, is strictly up to us. What we think of our age—how we feel about the number and what it represents—is totally subjective. We can celebrate our birthday, we can ignore our birthday, or we can simply note its appearance without changing our perception of what's possible.

AFFIRMATION: I will not be defined by my age.

*I experience the phenomenon of believing I am sweating
fifteen or twenty times a day or night.*

—George Sand

The operative word here is *believe*. Apparently George Sand,
writing in the nineteenth century, couldn't imagine the possibility that the hot flashes of menopause were real, physio-
logically based sensations and not just in her head.

Let's hope we no longer have to rationalize or apologize
for the symptoms of menopause or to pretend that they are a
figment of our imagination. That's enough to make anyone
feel crazy. And weak. And hypochondriacal (I could go on
and on).

Here's the deal, George: You weren't imagining anything.
We're not imagining anything. The first step toward acceptance is to believe what our body is telling us and to take
ourselves absolutely seriously in every respect.

AFFIRMATION: It's not in my head.

MONTH SIX   **DAY TWENTY-FIVE**

*To me, the cessation of my menstrual flow will be like
losing an old and valued friend.*
                                        —PELA SANDER

Do you remember back in high school using the euphemism
friend to describe your period? "My friend's here," we'd
whisper in code to a girlfriend. She'd nod in sympathy, and
we'd both giggle. Back then this was one friend we could
live without.

Now, as we anticipate or face the end of our menses, we
may suddenly feel sentimental. There *was* something com-
forting in the monthly appearance of our period, especially
in those panic-stricken moments when it was late and we
waited, hoping and praying for a trace of blood.

Whether we miss it or not, menopause means saying farewell to a familiar "friend" who was part of our lives for a
long, long time.

AFFIRMATION: Sometimes I miss getting my period.

I will swim. I will study tai chi. I will make my bones strong.

—KATHLEEN SIMS

There are numerous ways of battling osteoporosis, which is one of the most damaging and insidious side effects of menopause for some women.

Does swimming ten laps a day *really* make a difference? Will tai chi help? How about aerobics? Tums? Vitamin E?

Everything we do to be healthier, more fit, and more relaxed can't help but have a cumulative, curative effect. Is anything actually insurance against osteoporosis? Probably not. Until medical research catches up with menopause and its varying symptoms, we can try everything out there, keeping in mind that for now there's only so much we know and so much we can do.

AFFIRMATION: I will do what I can.

HOT FLASH: Eat more foods rich in Vita-
min D to help prevent osteoporosis.
—SUSAN PERRY AND KATHERINE A. O'HANLON,
M.D.

In their book *Natural Menopause* the authors recommend a daily dose of 400 IU (international
units) of vitamin D to ensure optimum calcium
absorption. In addition, some foods rich in calcium include skim milk, yogurt, turnip greens,
collards, broccoli, and sardines.

Most doctors and nutritionists agree that diet
plays an important role in preventing as well as
in slowing down the progress of osteoporosis.
The earlier we start thinking about it, the better
our chances of keeping our bones healthy and
strong.

If you haven't yet, it's time to take a proactive approach to fighting osteoporosis. Use the remaining space to describe your antiosteoporosis battle plan.

I will build healthy bones by . . .

MONTH SIX   **DAY TWENTY-NINE**

*Older women have been the midwives, herbalists, healers
and teachers in premodern societies.*

—MARVA KELSEA

As we enter the twenty-first century, we become more and
more appreciative of ourselves as wise women with magical,
mystical powers of healing.

Yet this is hardly a contemporary image. On the contrary,
it heralds a renaissance. Traditionally women in midlife have
been seen as the sacred dispensers of herbal medicine, spiritual guidance, wisdom, and power.

We need only look to the past, to our own heritage to
rediscover older women as the community's richest natural
resource, worthy of reverence and respect.

AFFIRMATION: Older women are wiser women.

The name "women of the fourteenth moon" came to me as I sought an honoring name for menopausal women.
—ELEANOR J. PICAZZA

"Simply, if there are thirteen full moons in a given year, a woman who has not had a period for a year will begin a new phase in her life upon the fourteenth full moon" continues this wonderfully positive essay included in the book by the same name.

This seems a fitting moniker for women whose menses have ceased. Our cycles are intrinsically connected to the phases of the moon. If in a given year there are thirteen full moons, what wild, transcendent experience might occur if we added one more? Frenzied dancing? Brilliant insights? Intense emotional shifts only available to those women fortunate enough to be part of this honorable, exclusive sisterhood?

AFFIRMATION: I am a woman of the fourteenth moon.

If you get six menopausal women together, you'll find that their doctors are doing six different things. You might as well go to a veterinarian.
— REPRESENTATIVE PATRICIA SCHROEDER

Well, maybe not a veterinarian. But the plethora of conflicting medical attitudes and antidotes for menopausal symptoms is confusing, making us wonder where to go, whom to trust, what course of treatment to follow in finding effective support.

The good news is we have a vast number of choices, which increases the odds of creating a customized plan that uniquely fits *your* needs.

The bad news is it's easy to feel overwhelmed. One doctor pushes HRT, another considers it a last resort, still another says the jury is still out and at best can only offer mixed reviews.

Ultimately it's up to us to be assertive, well-informed consumers, actively involved in figuring out the best course.

AFFIRMATION: I will make the effort to educate myself.

HYSTERECTOMY

*When you no longer have a uterus, how do you know if
you're going through the menopause?*

—CAROL PASCOE

Good question. And for those of us whose uterus has been
surgically removed through hysterectomy, the answer is ter-
ribly important.

Why? Because whether we've stopped menstruating or-
ganically or surgically, we still need to mark this passage in a
positive and meaningful way. Whether we're thirty, forty,
or fifty at the time of surgery, it's essential to stop and
acknowledge our menopause—not just as a physical shift but
as an emotional and spiritual change.

AFFIRMATION: I know by how I feel inside.

What do you do when you outlive your ovaries? Wear black underwear at half mast? Say Kaddish? Light Tampax votive candles?

—GAYLE SAND

Sarcasm aside, what *do* we do when we outlive our ovaries? Do we mourn the passing of our reproductive capacity? Although I can't imagine why we'd retire our black lacy underwear, I *can* understand the symbolism of saying Kaddish (the traditional Jewish mourning prayer) or creating some sort of meaningful ritual to mark this life-cycle passage and all it involves.

Tampax as a votive candle? Not a bad idea. Here are a few other possibilities:

- Create a ceremony with friends to affirm your passage into menopause
- Give away the baby clothes you've stored in the attic
- Plant a rosebush

AFFIRMATION: Ritual is another way of letting go.

EVOLUTION

Human women are the only creatures on earth to have menopause.

—JILL JEFFERY GINGHOFER

What an amazing bit of biological trivia! Whereas all other female species are reproductive throughout their lives, women are biologically wired to stop menstruating somewhere around age fifty-one. This made sense of course when women only lived until fifty or sixty, plenty of time to fulfill our roles as mothers.

Now, however, we may live until we're seventy, eighty, or ninety. Our life span has stretched, leaving us many more years in which to do all sorts of other things beside peopling the planet.

How do you want to spend the next twenty, thirty, or forty years?

AFFIRMATION: There are so many ways to fill my life.

If I were in Central America, the mother of a disap-
peared child, would I be feeling my menopausal symp-
toms?

—DENA TAYLOR

Maybe not. If we are to triage various life challenges—given
a life-threatening crisis—we'd likely be too distracted and
heartbroken to worry about hot flashes.

But that doesn't mean we wouldn't have them and it
doesn't mean that we're self-indulgent, in the absence of
worse problems, for paying attention to the very real experience of menopause. Feeling guilty, ashamed, or spoiled because we have the "luxury" of our pain doesn't help us *or*
those who are experiencing more profound suffering. We
can be sensitive to the misfortunes of others without negat-
ing our own feelings.

**AFFIRMATION: Each of us has our own particular
challenges to face.**

HOT FLASH: Make a contribution.

—Polly B.

On the other hand, as Polly, a forty-nine-year-old architect, points out, "We can forget about some of our problems by reaching out and helping those in need."

Midlife presents a rare opportunity to contribute our time to charitable causes. Any and every effort goes a long way, whether it's volunteering in a soup kitchen, fund-raising, cleaning up our neighborhood, or aiding the elderly.

Giving to others *does* take our minds off ourselves while making a much-needed contribution to our community.

Women in midlife who work for charitable causes say doing so helps alleviate symptoms and gives them a sense of satisfaction.

How would *you* like to lend a hand? If you are at a point in your life where you're ready to volunteer your services, write down your commitment here:

I am willing to . . .

Remember, anything you do—large or small—can make a real difference.

HONESTY

*At 53, I know I'm supposed to repeat the requisite chant
"I didn't get older, I got better" but . . .*
—FLORENCE KING

We may feel pressured to pay lip service to the positive,
upbeat mantras we've all heard regarding menopause and
aging. But what if we don't really mean it? What if, in fact,
they make us feel angry and discouraged, especially if we're
not feeling that way at all?

Better to accept our real feelings, even if they fly in the
face of Madison Avenue advertising slogans for collagen
creams and rehydrating lotions. Meanwhile how about coming up with an honest chant that truly reflects how you feel
about being in midlife? Maybe something like:

**AFFIRMATION: I am getting older and frankly I'm not
all that thrilled about it.**

The only advice I have for women in their forties is,
"Sit back, girl, and enjoy it! The worst is over. The best
is yet to come."

—ELENA FEATHERSTON

In other words we've struggled enough. We've earned the
right to sit back, rest on our past accomplishments, and truly
enjoy our lives.

For some of us this is easier said than done. We're used to
feeling as if everything is a fight; we're so used to having to
overcome obstacles, it's hard to imagine letting go and as-
suming a calmer, more relaxed attitude.

Perhaps the best *is* yet to come: a new decade in which we
can more easily handle the obstacles and take greater pleasure in the joys of life.

AFFIRMATION: I deserve to enjoy life.

AUTHENTICITY

To be a woman is to be an actress.

—SUSAN SONTAG

Midlife offers us the opportunity to become more outrageously, authentically ourselves.

As we get older, we're more able to drop the facade. We remove our mask, whether that means taking off our mascara, letting our hair shine silver, or wearing comfortable high-tops instead of wobbling around on high heels. We can stop saying our lines—the ones we've learned in order to get approval from our mothers, affection from our mates, admiration from co-workers or bosses.

When we stop acting, we start really being who we are. We make free choices. We can wear bright red lipstick, we can dress up, seduce, or charm, but we do it consciously, knowing who we are, what we're up to, and when it's time to step off the stage.

AFFIRMATION: I'm ready for the best role of my life: being myself.

*For myself it is a great relief not to be so motivated by
lust.*

—SANDY BOUCHER

It can be liberating to be relatively lust-free, as many women
in midlife will attest. If we accept rather than resent our
waning libido, we can focus energy on other creative pur-
suits. And the shift away from lust can be a great opening for
discovering other ways to be intimate with our mate.

Of course we may also experience lustlessness as a loss, in
which case it's important to find ways to get the sensual and
sexual nurturing we need. Here are some tried-and-true tips
from women in midlife:

- Take long baths with your lover
- Buy a vibrator
- Give—and receive—backrubs
- Don't panic—your libido will return in time

AFFIRMATION: These are natural ebbs and flows.

HEIGHTENED LIBIDO

I'm absolutely sure I'll have sex until I'm eighty.
—ISABEL ALLENDE

And as always, here's the flip side. For many women menopause releases a new surge of sexual energy. "My sexual appetite tripled," says Rita, age fifty-three. "I couldn't get enough, and my husband couldn't keep up with my insatiable libido," confides Samantha, age sixty-two. And lots of women describe lovemaking as more intense, their orgasms longer, deeper, and more satisfying than before menopause.

Yet another benefit. For those of us experiencing it, great! For those of us wondering if we'll ever want sex again, remember, this is a temporary phase that will likely change with time.

AFFIRMATION: Let's make love.

HOT FLASH: Buy new, sexy lingerie.

—LISA E.

That's one thing Lisa, a fifty-two-year-old mother and wife, did in an attempt to revitalize her lowered libido—a side effect, she says, that was one of the most frustrating aspects of being in menopause.

Whether you're feeling lustless or lusty, investing in new lingerie is a terrific way of affirming yourself right now. It's sort of like buying new sheets after getting divorced: a symbolic way of starting fresh.

Go ahead. Splurge on something lacy or sexy. Just as long as it's brand-new.

How is menopause affecting your sexuality? Is your libido heightened or lessened? Are your orgasms different than they were before?

In the following space complete this sentence: Since entering midlife, my sexuality has changed in these ways:

Now take a moment to reflect on how you feel about your changing sexuality.

I now realize that menopause is serious business.
>   —GRETA DARWICK

As women we've been conditioned to play down our experiences, to trivialize their significance and the meaning they have in our lives.

Menopause is a time when it's especially tempting to do so. We don't want to make a big deal out of it. We don't want to bore other people, be a burden on our family, be considered overwrought, overdramatic, or oversensitive, or any of the other *overs* we may be accused of as schemes for drawing attention to ourselves.

But menopause *is* serious business. It deserves our attention—without apology. Anything less is a great disservice to ourselves.

AFFIRMATION: I won't play down my menopause.

MOODINESS

> *Bounce a check, send back the main course, leave the house without make-up. No problem. Blame it on menopause.*
>
> —Gayle Sand

C'mon, Gayle!

Why take the easy way out? Why blame our carelessness, impatience, or sloppiness on menopause, a way of excusing or justifying less-than-acceptable behavior?

It might work, but doing so diminishes us. If we want respect, the last thing we need is to use menopause as a way of letting ourselves off the "hormone hook." On the contrary, midlife requires us to hold ourselves to our highest standards. We can expect the best of ourselves *and* accept our mood swings without sacrificing the support we need.

AFFIRMATION: I won't use menopause as a way out.

If you want to be functional at eighty, the time to start getting into shape is now.

—PETER D. WOOD

True enough advice. Getting in shape during midlife is money in the bank for being active and functional in later years.

However, I'd amend this statement to say: If you want to be functional at eighty *and* feel good today, the time to start getting into shape is now.

Eighty is just too far off for most of us to imagine. Working out so that we'll be spry some forty or fifty years from now isn't motivating enough to make most of us get off our rear ends and start making the effort to exercise. I'm for more immediate gratification. Getting in shape surely yields tangible rewards in the present, a more reasonable incentive to help us make, and stick to, a regular workout plan.

AFFIRMATION: I'm getting ready to get serious about getting in shape.

INDEPENDENCE

When you've been somebody's daughter, somebody's wife, somebody's mother, and now, you're just yourself, it's fabulous!

—PEG CURRAN

We spend a good portion of our lives defined in relation to others: I am Rosalie's younger daughter. Joey's wife. Zoe and Evan's mother. All of which bring me joy, but are only part of who I am.

We are more than the sum total of our relationships. And as we get older and stop defining ourselves this way, we are forced to look more deeply within to find out who we truly are. As individuals. As separate beings, first and foremost, who are capable of saying:

AFFIRMATION: Sometimes I give to others. And sometimes it feels fabulous to put myself first.

I decided that, by middle age, some things about me are never going to fundamentally change.
—FRANCES MOORE LAPPÉ

What a nice change *not* to be so fixated on changing and remaking ourselves.

We've spent so many years being self-critical, trying to improve our appearance and our abilities, doing everything imaginable to create a better, more polished and presentable version of ourselves.

But maybe this one's good enough. Maybe part of the pleasure of turning forty or fifty, is that we begin to accept ourselves. We reconcile our limitations and give ourselves a break.

This doesn't mean we let ourselves go; rather we take a healthier, more balanced and positive view of who we are.

AFFIRMATION: I don't need to try so hard.

HOT FLASH: Give yourself a break.
—Isabelle W.

These words of advice from Isabelle, age forty-seven, are important for each of us to hear.

She says, "The older I get, the less I push myself and the more I accept things about me that I used to worry so much about."

Most middle-aged women agree that self-acceptance is an essential step on the path to inner peace. Giving ourselves a break—learning to live with imperfect aspects of our personality—frees us to appreciate the ways in which we shine.

As you mature, you will notice ways in which you are coming to accept yourself. Little things—the birthmark you've always covered with makeup. And big things—the fact that you'll never be a brain surgeon or live in Jamaica year-round.

Write down five things about yourself that you are more accepting of these days:

1. _____
2. _____
3. _____
4. _____
5. _____

Come back to this page in six months and see what you can add to the list.

My mother's death made me realize how short life is.
— JUDITH KATZ

As we face our own aging, we also confront our parents' aging, and in some cases their death.

It's grievous to witness our parents—whom we once depended on for sustenance—now shrunken and frail, their gnarled hands and wizened faces a testimony to time's passage.

And as we mourn their eventual death, we catch a glimpse of our own mortality and recommit ourselves to making the most of every day ahead.

AFFIRMATION: Nothing is forever.

I don't take myself as seriously, and yet, I take who I am, dead seriously.

—GLORIA STEINEM

It's a paradox. As we mature, we gain greater perspective, ever more accepting of our imperfections, more forgiving of our flaws, more able to laugh at ourselves, knowing few things are as serious as they seem.

At the same time, we take our lives *more* seriously. We're unwilling to waste time or squander our energy. We pay closer attention to the lessons we're learning, the choices we're making, and the quality of our relationships, knowing that:

AFFIRMATION: Self-respect begins with how I treat myself.

PHYSICAL ACTIVITY

Even though I look older in the mirror, I still feel like running and skipping and jumping on a bike.

　　　　　　　　　　　　　　　　　　—KATE SHAW

Then by all means run and skip and jump on that bike for a brisk ride around the block!

The last thing we should do is to let our reflection in the mirror limit our physical activities. The more exercise we get—the more active we are—the better we feel.

Getting older is no excuse for falling into a sedentary lifestyle. If anything, exercise helps us feel younger and more vital.

AFFIRMATION: Let's go!

Having a woman as an elder and respecting her is so important.

—JEAN SHINODA BOLEN

I recently attended the bat mitzvah of my young friend and next-door neighbor, Molly. I've always been moved by the ancient Hebrew blessings, but what made this bat mitzvah so special were the words of Rabbi Marcie Zimmerman, who described Molly as a "wild woman" in the making, a wonderful affirmation from a respected elder to a young woman coming of age.

I'm glad Molly—and my daughter—have a female rabbi role model. And I'm just as grateful for the "elder" women who continue to emblazen the way, whether it's our mothers, an older friend, or a woman in our community whom we turn to for guidance.

AFFIRMATION: "Elder" women help pave the way.

MONTH SEVEN   **DAY TWENTY-SIX**

I am learning to become my own authority.
                                    —CATHLEEN ROUNTREE

As children we are taught to obey authority. As teenagers we learned to question authority. As younger women we have trusted other authorities—our parents, teachers, or spouses—rather than realizing that we are the ultimate source of truth.

As we fully come into our own, we begin to look within for the answers. We accept that while others may have much to give, there is no final authority, no absolute truth, beyond our own capacity to be discerning and wise.

AFFIRMATION: I am transferring authority to myself.

HOT FLASH: Trust yourself.

—NORA R.

What does it mean to trust ourselves?

According to Nora, who at age fifty-five left her husband for another woman, "it means being utterly honest about who we are, what we need, and acting on it despite the repercussions."

A tall order, whether it's trusting ourselves to change relationships, change careers, or change hair color. But it's one of the most important aspects of getting older, more confident, more willing to put ourselves on the line.

How have *you* started to trust your own gut and be more proactive in decision making?

In the following space write a short essay beginning with these words:

Upon entering midlife, I have found the inner confidence to . . .

Turning forty was great. It was the decade that I gave myself to public service.

—BARBARA BOXER

We give more *and* less as we age. On the one hand we're more protective of our time and energy, less willing to give and give until we've given ourselves away.

On the other hand as our spirituality deepens, we become more focused on what we truly value, and our generosity grows. We give willingly from our hearts. It's the difference between sacrifice and service, between giving to ease our guilt and giving because we're convinced it's the right thing to do.

AFFIRMATION: How can I be of service today?

> . . . *the closer I get to menopause, the more metaphysical I'm becoming.*
>
> —LILY TOMLIN AND JANE WAGNER

As we come into our prime, our priorities dramatically change. We are less concerned with material security and more aware of the mystical aspects of life. We experience an inner shift, from an emphasis on the ordinary to the extraordinary, deeply conscious that our daily acts are filled with purpose and meaning.

Becoming more spiritually attuned is manifested in many different ways; one woman in her forties commits to practice daily meditation, another joins a study group at her church, and still another makes a career change, trading the financial rewards of a corporate career for a more fulfilling position as a teacher of disabled children.

Perhaps as mortality becomes more of a reality, we naturally turn to spiritual sources for comfort and sustenance. It's another way we become richer, wiser human beings in the midstream of our life.

AFFIRMATION: As I mature, I have a deeper appreciation for magic and mysticism.

Margaret Thatcher, Eleanor Roosevelt, Golda Meir, Indira Gandhi all came into their own in the post-menopausal years.

—GAIL SHEEHY

Let's add Sandra Day O'Connor, Barbara Boxer, and Janet Reno to the list of prominent American midlife women in the public arena.

As we move into our forties and fifties, we're making policy, running corporations, affecting change at the highest levels, in the corridors of power where once only men's voices were heard.

We now have an abundance of extraordinarily powerful women leading the way. Whom do *you* admire and look up to? What midlife women give you inspiration and hope?

AFFIRMATION: My role model is . . .

DESEXUALIZATION

For most women, aging means a humiliating process of sexual disqualification.

—SUSAN SONTAG

Disqualified by whom? By the movies that portray female "sex objects," exclusively in their twenties or thirties? By the men who no longer flirt, leer, or make catcalls when we walk by? Or by our own selective perception of ourselves as no longer sexually interesting or appealing?

We must stop trying to compete against an image—which is really only something that we have been conditioned to believe—that youth and sexiness are one and the same. We mustn't rue the loss of sexual objectification that once defined and confirmed our feelings of self-worth.

Rather we must celebrate our more mature sensuality and sexuality that comes with knowing and loving our bodies and valuing ourselves—*not* as sex objects but as sexy, beautiful women, worthy of appreciation.

AFFIRMATION: I'm still a sexy and sexual human being.

Unfortunately I was taking my husband along for the ride. It was no longer my menopause. It was our menopause.

—GAYLE SAND

I think Gayle Sand's use of the word *unfortunate* is unfortunate. On the contrary, how very fortunate if we have a loving, trusting relationship with a mate who supports us in whatever ways he can. How fortunate for those of us who feel safe enough, loved enough, confident enough to turn to our partner without feeling ashamed or defensive about being in menopause.

It's just like pregnancy. We carry the baby, but we share the experience with our mate. In the same way, menopause can be a meaningful, mutual journey *if*—and it's a big *if*—we're willing to let him in.

AFFIRMATION: It's up to me to let him in.

UNCERTAINTY

It took me forty-four years to realize that all the answers aren't going to be settled.

　　　　　　　　　　　　　　　　　—MARIA VASQUEZ

The older we get, the more we know *and* the more we know that we *don't* know.

In other words we "get it" that life is mysterious and we stop feeling so anxious about having all the answers. We've learned, through experience, that there are few if any objective truths; what seemed clear at one stage evolves and changes over time.

There is a certain peace in accepting uncertainty. In learning to live with the gray areas. In realizing that the pursuit of truth raises yet more questions and that life itself is a process of ongoing inquiry.

AFFIRMATION: As I grow older, I accept that few things are black and white.

Many of us spend our first forty years learning the ways of the wounded, the next twenty we spend healing the wounds.

—CATHLEEN ROUNTREE

And the next twenty, hopefully, will be spent enjoying the blessed relief and freedom that comes from having confronted our pain and come out the other side.

Each of us has been wounded in different ways, as a result of neglect, abuse, or other trauma that has left a profound mark on our emotional makeup. And most of us have made a conscious effort to heal, through therapy or other means, so that now, in our forties and fifties, we can say:

AFFIRMATION: I have been hurt. I have healed. I am becoming whole.

HOT FLASH: See how far you've come.
—ELIZA B.

"In my twenties and thirties I was obsessed with working on all my issues," says Eliza, age forty-two. "I went to seminars, therapy, three different twelve-step groups, trying to recover from all the hurt I'd sustained in my childhood.

"It's not that everything's perfect now," she explains, "but since reaching my forties my focus has changed. I'm much less worried about ways in which I'm dysfunctional and much more aware of how healthy I am. Now," she continues, "instead of being in therapy, I say this one affirmation every morning: 'I am grateful for all the ways in which I am at peace.'"

It's a powerful statement. Seeing how far we've come is the next stage in the process of healing. Yet another midlife milestone to celebrate.

Acknowledging the ways in which we have and continue to heal is an important yardstick of emotional maturity. We needn't be all the way there— as we actively attend to remaining wounds—but, by the same token, we need and deserve to mark our progress: the ways in which we are less self-destructive, aspects of our relationships that are healthier and more fulfilling, old behavioral patterns that we no longer revert to in times of stress.

In what ways are you conscious of your own healing? In the following space claim your own growth by completing this sentence:

I've come a long way in these areas:

*I needed a magic pill that would help **me** become balanced again.*

—GRETA DARWICK

Some say estrogen is *the* magic pill, the menopausal woman's equivalent to Prozac for depression—an instant cure and painless antidote to the various symptoms we experience in midlife.

For some women estrogen indeed turns out to be the answer. Others struggle with dosage, side effects, and fear of potential long-term health risks.

In truth we're still a long way from finding a "magic pill." Meanwhile we experiment with the limited resources available, trying to find the right balance that will restore the greatest degree of comfort and relief.

AFFIRMATION: I accept that there are no simple answers.

MONTH EIGHT   **DAY NINE**

*I spent thirty years, maybe forty years, never having a
day off.*

—MAXINE HONG KINGSTON

This is one statement I hope few readers will identify with.
Thirty or forty years without one day off? What's with this
woman? I can barely imagine how exhausted she must be!

Thank goodness she's realizing it's time to make a change.
God knows, we all need days off to rest, regroup, and
recharge our batteries. For those of us who have always built
in vacations or "mental health days," keep it up! For anyone
who hasn't, better late than never.

If you do one thing for yourself to celebrate your next
birthday, make it this:

AFFIRMATION: I promise to take time for myself.

There's more intelligence, more heart, more warmth as I get older.

—DEENA METZGER

All right! More examples of ways in which we improve as we get older.

It makes sense. We should be smarter, considering all the education and information that has naturally refined our intellectual capability. Our heart, compassion, and humanity should be deepened as we've lived long enough to have sustained wounds as well as experienced all the love and kindness we've received.

We may, however, not even be aware of the ways in which we've gotten better. Stop for a moment and think of three ways in which you've improved with age. If you can't come up with anything, ask a trusted friend to share his or her input.

AFFIRMATION: With age I've become more . . .

Month Eight   **Day Eleven**

*I nourish myself with meditation, psychotherapy, garden-
ing, walking.*

—Maxine Hong Kingston

These are four excellent ways of relaxing and of replenishing
ourselves.

Meditation: a personal discipline in which we focus on our
breathing and become still enough to hear our deep inner
voice.

Psychotherapy: a courageous journey through which we
unearth our demons, confront our pain, build on our
strengths, and develop new strategies for handling stress.

Gardening: a partnership with nature through which we
get in touch with the cosmic cycles.

And walking, which gets our heart pumping, our energy
flowing, our head cleared so that we can cope with the
demands of daily life.

How do you nourish yourself?

AFFIRMATION: I nourish myself by . . .

COMPANIONSHIP

*As you get older, things happen to you and around you:
death, sickness; and it's nice to have someone to face
them with.*

—JUDY CHICAGO

Stories abound of women in midlife spreading their wings
and taking flight from their marriages in order to pursue
greater freedom and independence.

But there's also a lot to be said for companionship, for
having someone with whom to share the ups and downs, the
adversity and the joy, the mundane realities along with the
more profound challenges we face as we age.

That someone may be a lover or a spouse. Or it may be a
dear, dear friend. What matters is to know there's someone
there over the long haul.

**AFFIRMATION: I am grateful for the support in my
life.**

HOT FLASH: Don't take anyone who loves
you for granted.

—GAIL N.

Always good advice, I was struck by how often
women in midlife made a point of mentioning the
importance of tending and nourishing our most
intimate relationships.

"We've always had a pretty good marriage, but
now, in my fifties, I'm keenly aware of how precious love is and how easily it is to lose our connection if I don't actively nurture it," says Gail,
whose youngest son recently started college.
"Now, more than ever, I'm committed to Steven. I
realize that he's the one who will be at my side
for whatever years remain."

The older we get, the more we treasure our
loved ones, grateful for our shared history and
enduring devotion.

Midlife offers us a renewed opportunity to evalu-
ate our relationships and to recommit to them in
a new and deeper way.

Take a moment now to think about the special
people in your life: your mate, children, friends.
What new relationships have you cultivated in
the past five years? Where do you turn for comfort and support? Who will be near and dear as
you enter the next decade of your life?

Now ask yourself this question: Am I doing everything possible to nurture these relationships?

I feel like I'm fifteen at the drugstore buying my first Kotex.

—GAYLE SAND

Or my first birth control pills. Or my first pregnancy test. Or my first K-Y vaginal cream—yet another somewhat embarrassing and uncomfortable public acknowledgment that we are indeed in menopause.

Firsts can be exciting. Markers of a whole new world of experience ahead. Yet they can also be a relatively uncomfortable reality check, something we aren't quite ready for but is here nonetheless.

Like any first it gets easier as it goes.

AFFIRMATION: I'm getting there.

> *"Maybe women should leave their husbands," I say, "instead of taking drugs."*
> —AMBER COVERDALE-SUMRALL

Rubbish! Besides, it's just a temporary solution to momentarily ease our frustration until we miss our husband (however imperfect) and wish he was back at our side.

No, getting rid of him as a way of coping with menopausal symptoms strikes me as a lousy idea, unless of course our marriage is crumbling, in which case we need professional counseling, not a quick fix.

On the contrary, we need to work *with* our partner, actively educating him as to what we are going through. We need to turn to him for comfort, grateful for his support, even in our worst moments when we're tempted to push him away.

AFFIRMATION: I'll show him how to support me.

In your forties you suddenly are part of the older generation.

—SUSAN GRIFFIN

Last night, after hearing writer and charter member of the sixties' generation Paul Krassner speak at a local bookstore, my son, Evan, asked, "Mom, what's 'the establishment'?"

I stumbled for the right words: "It's the government . . . it's the people who tell you what's normal, what's the right and acceptable way to behave."

"Oh, I get it," he replied. "You're *my* establishment."

God, no! I wanted to scream. *I'm young! Rebellious! I'm still a hippie protesting the Vietnam War.*

But to my son I'm part of the older generation. I pay taxes, I go to the PTA. I rarely make it to *David Letterman.*

Does that make me old? Relatively speaking, yes. I guess it depends on whom you ask.

AFFIRMATION: I still consider myself young.

Dance allows women to go deep within themselves.
—ARISIKA RAZAK

As does drumming. And throwing clay. And baking bread, along with countless other creative endeavors.

Last year I attended a women's retreat. Saturday night's activity was line dancing; imagine a hundred women, ages twenty-two to seventy-two, bandannas around our necks, kicking and shaking to Achy Brakey with utter abandon and joy. Some of us had the steps down, others stumbled, and often we knocked into one another, which had us in stitches.

In some ways being in midlife makes it harder to dance or drum or fly around the kitchen, especially if we're not in the habit of letting loose. We feel embarrassed. Intimidated. Afraid of looking stupid or foolish.

If we can get beyond our fear, we find new ways of throwing ourselves fully into what we love, losing ourselves in the rhythm of our passion.

AFFIRMATION: I will express myself freely and joyously.

I don't spend much time thinking about what I might have done, because I did what I wanted to do.

—JUDY CHICAGO

It's a common refrain. Most of us feel some degree of regret as we contemplate our choices. "I should have left that marriage years before." "I wish I'd put off my career instead of putting my children in day care." "I might have been an actress if I hadn't been brought up to think I had to be a teacher."

In fact what we *might* have been doesn't mean a thing. For whatever reasons—emotional or economic—we made choices that seemed right then; in the cosmic unfolding each of us did *exactly* what was right when we were twenty or thirty or forty. We can't turn back the clock. But there's nothing stopping us now!

Rather than wallowing in regret, we can commit ourselves full-force to what we want to do today.

AFFIRMATION: I will resurrect my dreams.

HOT FLASH: Regret nothing.

—BETSY T.

In the best of all possible worlds perhaps Betsy's advice would hold true. It would be wonderful to live our lives without any regret, without any wishes or should-haves or might-have-been-if-only-I'd-done-this-instead-of-that.

Realistically few of us are entirely regret-free. We've all made choices that—having had more information, courage, or resources—we wouldn't make today.

Perhaps there's another way of dealing with our feelings of regret: by acknowledging our sadness and disappointments so that we can get beyond them and free ourselves to make new, fresh choices. Facing the past is one of midlife's assignments. Staying stuck in regret is paralyzing; grieving empowers us to act.

Here's an exercise that's helpful in coping with feelings of regret:

1. Make an honest list of every regret of which you are aware, using the words, "I wish I had" or "I'm sorry I didn't."

2. After reading each statement of regret, allow yourself a moment to experience any feelings of sadness, guilt, or remorse.

3. Now, after each statement of regret, write down the sentence "I did my best then. I'm ready to forgive myself."

4. Finally, compose a second list, this one expressing new commitments you are willing to make that reflect who you are today, in the present. For example if you write down "I wish I had spent more time with my children," after completing steps 2 and 3 create a new statement, such as, "I commit to spending more time with my children starting today."

As you complete this exercise, remember that you are a human being who is allowed to make mistakes *and* allowed to correct them over time.

ACCEPTANCE

We must accept aging, not just accept but insist that aging is beautiful.

—MAXINE HONG KINGSTON

Some aspects of aging aren't so easy to accept: the diminishment of energy; physical aches and pains; the wrinkles we wouldn't necessarily choose, much less embrace.

It's fine to say we should transform our perceptions of aging as beautiful, but how do we go about it?

We do it by noticing other women of the same age, admiring their lines of character, the strength in their carriage, the depth in their eyes. And we do it by looking at ourselves and saying, every single day:

AFFIRMATION: I am growing into a more beautiful person.

MONTH EIGHT   **DAY TWENTY-THREE**

*Since hot flashes are often cryptic, I try to decipher their
meaning as soon as possible.*

—BARBARA RASKIN

In her novel, *Hot Flashes,* author Barbara Raskin describes
spontaneous flashes of insight as a positive side effect of
menopause.

She's not alone. Many women report that in the flash, or a
flush, they experience new awareness, sometimes in the
form of visions, dreams, conveying messages too urgent to
ignore.

Maybe that's what it means to "hear voices." We're not
crazy, we're just more attuned to another level of reality, a
deeper level of consciousness in which we're highly receptive
to our own inner voice.

AFFIRMATION: I'll tune in.

ALTERNATIVE TREATMENTS

I had tried everything from age-old ayurveda, acupuncture, herbs, new-age crystals, healing and aromatherapy.
— GAYLE SAND

These alternative remedies are actually age-old, traditional antidotes that many women in menopause are experimenting with as a way of lessening their symptoms.

While they may not be a panacea, it's worth exploring everything that's out there. We needn't be intimidated by "new age" options nor overly dazzled by their promises.

If crystals make hot flashes easier to handle, why not? If drinking ginseng helps the mood swings, go for it!

It needn't be all or nothing. We can take the best of natural "cures" along with Western medicine, striking an effective balance between the two.

AFFIRMATION: I'll try to have an open mind.

I'm now free to do certain things that I wouldn't have if I'd had children.

—LINDA LEONARD

Linda Leonard, author of *On the Way to the Wedding,* goes on to say, "But as I get older, it seems to be more of a loss."

It's a mixed blessing. Those of us who are child-free may feel quite right about the decision, while others experience twinges of regret. On the one hand, now that we're in midlife, we aren't facing the challenges of growing children, college bills, and motherhood. On the other hand we may be haunted by what we've missed. We wonder how our lives would have been different. We may be acutely aware that as we age, we won't have sons and daughters to care for us down the road.

We've all made trade-offs. Hopefully, on balance, our fulfillment outweighs any lingering regret.

AFFIRMATION: I will make the most of how my life has turned out.

I'd like to grow very old as slowly as possible.
—IRENE MAYER SELZNICK

At ten, summer vacation seemed an eternity. At twenty, menopause seemed light-years away. At forty or fifty or sixty, time begins to close in, each day, sunup to sundown, is shortened; the more aware we are of time passing, the faster it seems to go.

Perhaps we can slow down our experience of time if we can recapture how we felt as children. When the present moment was everything, when a melting ice-cream cone consumed our attention and nothing else mattered. Perhaps if we stop being so worried about what's coming—about how much time has passed and how little remains—we can live in the present instead of racing after time.

AFFIRMATION: I will try to slow down.

HOT FLASH: Revise your negative precon-
ceptions of aging.

—Rhoda W.

"My women's group has really helped me to fashion a better concept of what it means to be in my
fifties," says Rhoda, whose career is devoted to
caring for terminally ill cancer patients in a hos-
pice. "Whereas I used to think getting older
meant inevitable decline," continues Rhoda,
"now I spend lots of time with other incredibly
vital women in their mid-years, which has really
turned around how I see myself."

As Rhoda has learned, it's up to us to revise
our negative perceptions, replacing them with
more positive images of aging. We can be realistic, we can prepare ourselves, we can cope with
what comes without falling into a negative frame
of mind. The choice is ours.

The writer Anaïs Nin said, "We don't see things as they are, we see things as *we* are."

Roughly interpreted, this means that how we frame our reality has a big impact on what we feel.

Aging is a perfect example of this. We can nurse negative images or we can focus on cultivating a more positive attitude. The first step is to identify the belief systems that inform our experience.

Take a moment now to examine any negative concepts you attach to aging. In the following space, complete this sentence as many times as you choose:

The worst thing about getting older is . . .

Now look closely at your beliefs. Is there anything you can do to shift to a more positive mindset?

> *I loved it when Blacks had the slogan, "Black is beautiful."*
>
> —MAXINE HONG KINGSTON

How inspiring to transform damaging stereotypes into gloriously empowering statements of pride.

We can do the same for the spirit of aging, redefining our cultural perception to see midlife and maturity as a beautiful and exciting stage of life that can and should be treated with reverence.

Let's begin by creating a worthy slogan to celebrate women in midlife. How about "Forty and fabulous"? "Fifty and full of life"?

Now it's your turn. What would you like to see on a banner or T-shirt or bumper sticker? Give it a shot:

AFFIRMATION: My slogan is . . .

Thank God I finished breast-feeding just in time for menopause.

—"Sondra," quoted by Gail Sheehy

We may be nursing babies with a fan in hand. Or weaning them just as we're beginning to wonder whether our period's gone for good. Or coming to terms with a decision not to have more children just as the decision is being taken out of our hands.

If this weird, synchronistic hormonal timing is happening to you, let yourself experience all your feelings. Grieve the end of one stage of life so that you can experience—in all its richness—the beginning of the next.

AFFIRMATION: I will consciously mark each new stage of life.

You want a hot woman? This is a hot woman!
—GAYLE SAND

This is my single, favorite line from Gayle Sand's book, *Is It Hot in Here or Is It Just Me?*

Hot doesn't just mean "sweaty, flushed, uncomfortable from menopausal hot flashes." But *hot!* "Sexy, sensual, up for an erotic adventure."

The next time a hot flash makes you feel crummy, try seeing yourself this way: as a steamy, sizzling, sexy woman who's *hot* in the best sense of the word.

AFFIRMATION: I am a hot woman.

PERSPECTIVE

Now I know what deserves attention, completion and commitment and what is a passing idea that doesn't deserve a place setting at the table.

—BARBARA HAMM

We are more focused than ever, clearer about which relationships, projects, family, and community involvements require—and deserve—our absolute, undivided attention.

And as we focus, we're less drained and distracted by fleeting fantasies, less easily seduced and engaged by what falls outside our fundamental goals.

All of which leaves us with greater energy to do what's truly important, what truly feeds our soul.

AFFIRMATION: I refuse to spread myself too thin.

I'm going on a cruise to the Bahamas, but before I do,
I'm going to get me a liposuction.

—TRUDY RILEY

A cruise to the Bahamas (if we can afford it) is a great way for midlife women to indulge ourselves in a luxurious escape.

And a liposuction (if we can afford it) is a great way for *some* midlife women to enhance our self-image and give ourselves a real treat.

Both are expensive; neither is the only way to escape or pamper ourselves. For some women cosmetic surgery is a terrific option, while others find the idea distasteful, morally objectionable, or simply out of the question. Let me go on record as making no value judgments. This is a personal choice, right for some of us, wrong for others.

Meanwhile there are lots of other ways to take a temporary vacation—a long soak in the bathtub, a gift certificate (ask for one for your next birthday) at a local day spa, a weekend away with a few of our favorite women friends— can go a long way toward giving us a new lease on life.

AFFIRMATION: An occasional treat is a must for my mental health.

SILENCE

> *The Silent Passage* made it onto the list of the ten
> most shoplifted books in America.
>
> —GAIL SHEEHY

Wow! This piece of literary trivia says so much about so
many different aspects of menopause: (a) that huge numbers
of women are experiencing it and will go to great lengths—
albeit illegal ones—to get their hands on a book about it; (b)
that we're too embarrassed about menopause to step up to a
counter in a bookstore or check this book out of the library;
and (c) that we need up-to-date, inexpensive, easily accessi-
ble information on menopause.

All of the above make one thing clear: Menopause is here.
It's happening to lots of us. We need to stop feeling shy
about it and make sure we get all the information we can get
our hands on.

AFFIRMATION: I have nothing to hide.

I think teaching is right for wise middle-aged women.
                                    —MAXINE HONG KINGSTON

Teaching—whether in the role of mother, mentor, or college professor—is one of the most rewarding steps in the journey from youth to age. We owe it to ourselves and to others to pass on the benefit of our experience. It's both an honor and an obligation to inspire, educate, and guide those who are a few steps farther back on the road.

And it is deeply gratifying. As we teach, we realize how much we know. We enjoy the profound satisfaction that comes from enlightening others with our knowledge and wisdom.

AFFIRMATION: I have so much to give.

HOT FLASH: Pass on your wisdom.

—Dianne E.

"The biggest shift I've experienced since turning forty-five is seeing how much I have to teach others," says Dianne, a single mother and legal secretary, who recently started a weekly support group for adolescent girls. "I'm not an expert," she's quick to point out, "but I've realized that after raising two daughters alone, I have something to give in this area."

It's a matter of confidence. In our forties and fifties we come to trust our wisdom and place a greater value on our skills. And we find the guts to take on the mantle of mentor, teacher, and guide with a firm belief in all we have to offer.

Are *you* ready to pass on the wisdom and knowledge you've gained over the past forty or fifty years?

One woman in midlife, whose hobby was watercolor painting, placed an ad in the community-college newsletter and began offering classes on the weekends. Another volunteered at her local family and children's service as a "big sister" to a fourteen-year-old girl who had recently been through treatment for chemical dependency. Yet another went through training to do peer counseling through her church, her first step toward going back to school in her fifties and becoming a clinical psychologist.

There are many, many different ways of teaching, mentoring, or guiding others in areas in which we excel.

What knowledge, talent, or skills have you developed? Can you think of at least one way in which you can begin teaching others what you know?

Try completing the following two sentences:

1. I have become an "expert" at . . .
2. I can pass on my expertise by . . .

Menopause happens to every single woman.
—ELLEN SUE STERN

All women experience menopause. We may be forty, fifty, or sixty; black, white, or brown; rich, poor, or somewhere in between. Unlike pregnancy, which we may or may not go through, menopause is a natural and inevitable part of every woman's life.

But the experience itself differs vastly from one woman to the next. Some battle with hot flashes, some keep asking what they're like. Some ride an emotional roller coaster, others say it's smooth sailing all the way. Each of us has her own perfectly valid, totally unique experience. We feel solidarity, which doesn't mean uniformity. We can empathize without mirroring one another's reality.

AFFIRMATION: We all experience menopause in our own way.

After fifty most of the bullshit is gone.
—ISABEL ALLENDE

This simple, no-bullshit statement says it like it is.

For the sake of argument, let's define *bullshit* as ''anything and everything that erodes our integrity and diminishes our power,'' including: the endless ways we accommodate others by saying what we think *they* want to hear, doing what we think would make *them* happy, being what we think would gain *their* love and approval.

The end to compromising our beliefs, cutting corners off our personality, capitulating, controlling or censoring ourselves means the beginning of saying—and meaning:

AFFIRMATION: This is who I am. Take it or leave it.

MORTALITY

Part of my fantasy of aging has been destroyed by my sister's death.

—COKIE ROBERTS

"I always thought she'd be in the rocking chair next to me," ABC News special correspondent goes on poignantly to say.

It is a rude and heartbreaking awakening to witness the death of our siblings or friends, especially those in their forties or fifties. When cancer or heart disease or other misfortune robs us of a loved one in his or her mid-years, our own mortality hits us between the eyes. If it can happen to them, it can happen to us. Our own aging becomes that much more palpable.

On the positive side, the death of a peer may also inspire us to reassess our own lives; to become more conscious of our choices, more aware of our spirituality, more grateful for what we have.

AFFIRMATION: My mortality is becoming more real to me.

I think "Wow" I had such a great body when I was
younger—I didn't appreciate it.

—NATALIE GOLDBERG

There's a famous saying: Youth is wasted on the young.

In so many ways we took ourselves for granted—our boundless energy, our attractiveness; the opportunities that were open to us in our twenties and thirties.

In retrospect we realize how good we had it. But it's all relative. At age eighty we may think, "Wow, I had so many friends around when I was seventy." At seventy we may say, "I was in so much better health when I was sixty." At sixty we may say, "I had so much more disposable income when I was fifty."

Rather than wistfully wishing we were younger, the trick is to be aware of all the ways in which our lives are pleasurable and fulfilling right now. Today.

AFFIRMATION: Today I am appreciative of . . .

DISILLUSIONMENT

To live fifty years is to confront inescapable truths about life.

—AUDREY BORENSTEIN

Some say we become disillusioned with age.

But disillusionment can be an enlightening and, yes, empowering experience. As we mature, we face any number of inescapable truths: that our children are slowly—and appropriately—less and less dependent on us. That our career choices are pretty much decided, that our relationships may or may not be all that we hoped for, that our health is bound to diminish, that we aren't going to live forever, and that the world is an imperfect place that we have a limited capacity to change.

Sound depressing? Not necessarily. There is great peace in trading our illusions for reality, in reconciling our fantasies with a saner—and more reachable—picture of what is possible.

AFFIRMATION: Facing the truth is a necessary step toward sanity.

HOT FLASH: Embrace the truth.

—TERESA Q.

"For years I've had the saying The Truth Will Set You Free taped to my refrigerator. But it's only since turning forty that I've come to understand what it means," says Teresa.

In Teresa's case, embracing truth meant two things: accepting the reality that her father was never going to give her the love and attention she wanted, and, realizing that the "perfect man" she'd been searching for in her twenties and thirties simply didn't exist.

Facing the truth *is* liberating; it frees us to stop being angry and frustrated about what we can't change and concentrate on the areas of life where we can truly make a difference.

What illusions have *you* stripped away over the past ten years? What hard truths have you confronted, either about yourself, others, or the state of the world?

In the following space compose a short essay entitled "I Have No More Illusions About . . ." Or simply consider the question and see what comes up for you.

Once you've completed this assignment, ask yourself, How has my life improved as a result of facing these truths? Notice ways in which facing the truth has set you free.

It is not our uterus but our heart that is our real womb.
—MARIANNE WILLIAMSON

New-age guru Marianne Williamson goes on to pose the challenge "Our real question must be this: What do we want to give birth to?"

Many of us have been actively asking ourselves this for a long time, actively searching for ways in which to manifest our creativity and midwife our dreams.

As mothers we've literally had the opportunity to do so. But as women, especially once our womb is no longer the vehicle for our creative urges, we find other, equally fulfilling, ways to give birth: through artistic expression. Through acts of charity and kindness. We channel our desires into continual acts of creation that come straight from the heart.

AFFIRMATION: My heart is the source of my creativity.

STIGMA

People talk about turning forty as though it were akin to having your wisdom teeth removed.

—Anna Quindlen

What's the deal? Why do so many of us wince or waffle when the subject of our fortieth birthday comes up?

I'm no different. A recent call from my mother asking how I'd like to spend my fortieth revealed my own ambivalence: "I don't know," I muttered, adding, "I'm not sure I want to do anything about it. Can't it just come and go without making a fuss?"

This is radically different from how I approached my thirtieth birthday: With great anticipation I planned a party of all my friends and reveled in the attention.

Maybe we've been contaminated by all the cultural propaganda. Remember the slogan "I'd rather be pregnant than forty"? As if, being forced to choose between the lesser of two evils, morning sickness wins out any day over midlife.

It's up to us to transform the experience of turning forty from a dreaded event to a cause for celebration. I, for one, am in the process of planning a party for March 13th.

AFFIRMATION: I will turn forty with joy.

> *The point is not to give up on beauty and fitness, but to give up on self-loathing.*
>
> —SUSAN POWTER

Powter, the recent sensation whose slogan is "Stop the insanity," is right on the money.

She's selling self-empowerment: the idea that it is our personal responsibility to do everything possible to feel better about ourselves. Most of us would benefit from listening. Even those of us who are relatively comfortable with our appearance have had to struggle with insecurity and self-loathing. We're too fat or too thin, our hair's too limp or too wild, our nose is too narrow or too pointed; each of us can list our imperfections—the particular flaws that keep us from being beautiful.

But we are beautiful. Fashion models? Not necessarily. But beautiful all the same. No one—not our husband, not our friends, not a therapist—can convince us to stop the insanity of judging ourselves against impossibly unattainable standards. Only we can look in the mirror and say:

AFFIRMATION: I am a perfectly beautiful woman.

WEIGHT GAIN

Middle age is when your age starts to show around your middle.

—BOB HOPE

A friend of mine (who will remain anonymous) recently confided that, for all her effort, she can't drop the extra eight pounds that showed up in her fortieth year and seems insistent on staying, regardless of what she eats or how much she exercises.

It's a constant refrain. Women in midlife complain that everything's a little lower, our stretch marks more visible, and that it's harder to keep off the pounds. We wear looser apparel, vertical stripes, darker colors to camouflage the unwelcome spread.

No matter how great we feel about being in midlife, we may still miss the sleeker, tighter body we once had. Midlife is filled with loss and gains. This is one of the inevitable losses. In turn we gain a more accepting, less perfectionistic view of ourselves.

AFFIRMATION: I don't have to like it.

Seems the journal is the menopausal woman's repository of questions.

—GRETCHEN SENTCHEN

And musings . . . and feelings . . . and reflections on all the myriad psychic and emotional shifts midlife brings up.

If you've always kept a journal, great! Make the commitment to write in it daily, recording both the ups and the downs you're experiencing as a result of menopause.

If you haven't yet, then this is an opportune time to buy yourself a journal. It can be a simple ninety-eight-cent spiral notebook or a beautifully bound hardcover book with women's quotes on each page to inspire your writing.

It doesn't have to be anything fancy. What matters is to keep an ongoing account to share or keep private, to look back on as a personal keepsake of this passage.

AFFIRMATION: I have so much to say.

HOT FLASH: Every woman in midlife
should keep a daily journal.

—ROBERTA A.

Should is a pretty strong word, but other than
that, Roberta, a fifty-two-year-old trust officer, has
good reason for believing that a journal is an essential companion for women in midlife.

"I started when I was forty and I've been writing
in mine every morning," she says. "Without being
overly dramatic, it's the single thing that's kept
me sane."

Even if you do it once a week or once a month,
keeping a journal is a wonderful gift to give yourself. The following renewal worksheet will help
you get started.

Here are some guidelines for keeping a midlife journal:

1. Invest in a notebook or journal that's strictly used for this purpose.
2. Date each entry.
3. Be as honest and un-self-censoring as possible.
4. Remember, this is *just* for you. Only share it with those you trust.

Now, here are a few suggested topics to help jump-start your creative juices:

- A. Ways in which midlife has altered my body image and sexuality.
- B. How my personal relationships are being affected by menopause.
- C. Old feelings, fears, and issues midlife is bringing up for me.
- D. Letters to my child from this new stage of life.

Or you may simply fill in the blank pages with any feelings, impressions, and insights. Anything and everything you write is valid and worthwhile.

MOURNING

*Every time I see a pregnant woman I get mourning
sickness.*

—GAYLE SAND

For women who have remained child-free such as Gayle
Sand, menopause may evoke pain as we grieve the lost possibility of pregnancy and motherhood.

In contrast, for those of us with growing or grown children, the sight of a pregnant woman evokes a mixture of
gratitude and grief. We remember too well the morning
sickness, swollen ankles, every single contraction from transition to crowning. Perhaps the sight of a pregnant woman is
a litmus test for where we're at. Those of us who have not
had children may feel twinges of regret. Those of us who are
mothers may be glad that's in the past.

**AFFIRMATION: The sight of a pregnant woman makes
me feel . . .**

The classic medical terminology for menopause is ovarian failure. Another way of saying it is "ovarian fulfillment."

—GAIL SHEEHY

We're not mincing words here. What we call things profoundly affects how we experience them.

It's time to put a new spin on menopause. Rather than perceiving it as ovarian failure—as an inability to produce eggs—why not see menopause as the long-awaited culmination wherein our reproductive capacity has fulfilled its destiny.

Having reached this stage, we are filled with a deep sense of satisfaction. And we are freed to take on new tasks, new ways of manifesting our creativity in this next stage of the journey.

AFFIRMATION: I am fulfilled.

MONTH NINE   DAY TWENTY-FOUR

There are a few good things about turning fifty, like becoming a first-time grandmother.
                                    —DORIS BIRCHAM

Another midlife benefit to add to the "plus" column.

Although fewer women in their fifties are becoming grandmothers as their daughters are postponing pregnancy, there are still plenty who enjoy this most pleasurable perk of midlife. As FiftySomething grandmothers we're young enough to have energy to play with and baby-sit our beloved grandchildren. And we're still close enough to the experience of our own motherhood to pass on some wisdom, which, if done graciously, can be a great gift and way of connecting with grown children.

Most women say being a grandmother is much easier and more fun than being a mother. We relax and savor the tangible fruits of our labor.

AFFIRMATION: I can't wait.

Age does not protect you from love. But love, to some extent, protects you from age.

—JEANNE MOREAU

It's true. A woman "in love" appears relatively ageless. Her eyes are radiant, her skin aglow with anticipation. There's a spring in her walk, a sparkle in her smile.

To be sure, as we age we are no less vulnerable to the difficulties of love—the disappointments and the sorrows, the losses and the lessons. But we give and receive with greater ease that comes of having loved before, only this time, with more wisdom and maturity. If anything, being in love is a greater gift the older we get.

AFFIRMATION: I'm never too old to feel in love.

COMMUNICATION

Tom thought I was nuts. He didn't feel any surge of heat under the bedclothes.

—Clara Felix

The climate wars! A recurring battle between bedmates, one of whom is shivering while the other is steaming from yet another hot flash.

Is this an inevitable casualty of menopause? Sometimes. Is there anything we can do to ease this issue or alleviate it altogether?

Yes. Separate blankets (one off, one on), an electric blanket with his/her switches, light nightclothes, and fans are all ways of combatting the climate wars. (Separate beds are a last resort, best used as temporary intervention.)

Most importantly we need to keep this fight from escalating into full-scale war and/or masking other, more significant relationship issues.

If you're really fighting over the thermostat, stop and find some creative, cooperative solution.

If, however, you're fighting about something else, come clean and deal with the underlying problems before things really heat up.

AFFIRMATION: I will find creative solutions to the climate wars.

HOT FLASH: Talk, talk, talk to your husband!

—ESTHER C.

I know. We all wish he could read our mind, that he'd ask how we're doing and bring in the cooler and tell what heroes we are in handling our hot flashes, but it's probably not going to happen. At least not often enough to make him the ideal menopausal mate.

So here's the alternative: Tell him what you need. Clearly, calmly, without threatening or throwing a fit. Or as Esther, a forty-nine-year-old physicist whose husband's constant criticism of her constant tossing and turning drove her to sleep on the couch, simply puts it, "Spell it out if you have to. Say, look, this is hard enough for me without having to apologize for my hot flashes. Please help me get through this instead of making it worse."

Sometimes it works. Sometimes it requires a fair amount of finesse. But we need to keep telling him what we need if we're ever going to get it.

MONTH NINE   **DAY TWENTY-EIGHT**

Communication is an essential ingredient in smooth-running relationships, and it's never more true than now.

Are *you* talking to your mate, explaining how you feel and asking for his support? Or are you angry and resentful, waiting and waiting for him to come through?

You're not responsible for his lack of support. You are, however, responsible for spelling out what you need. If you haven't, on the next few lines write down, in the form of requests, what you'd like to ask your mate for in the way of support:

1. _____

2. _____

3. _____

Some forms of madness are no more than failed transitions from one vision of life to the next.

—SHELDON KOPP

This profound definition of madness rings true on many different levels, all of which are pertinent to midlife.

If we fail to acknowledge this transition as a physical, emotional, and spiritual pilgrimage, we remain stuck, hanging in midair between the past and the present.

If we fail to create a vision of the woman we will grow into over the next five, ten, and twenty years, we stumble aimlessly, without a compass to guide us on our path.

In order to navigate a smooth and sane transition, we need to say with conviction:

AFFIRMATION: I know where I've been. I know where I am. I know where I'm going.

> *I felt guilty about choosing HRT because it seemed I was cheating on other women.*
>
> —PAT RHODA

Wow. Women will feel guilty over just about anything!

I hear it again and again. From expectant mothers who worry they've copped out by having an epidural instead of a medication-free childbirth. From mothers who work outside the home who are defensive over having live-in child care despite grueling schedules and less than adequate financial resources. And now from women who, often after much soul-searching, feel guilty about choosing estrogen over "natural remedies," who feel they've let down the sisterhood in their effort to slow down the visible aging process while others get wrinkled and gray.

It's codependence at its best and its worst. It's to our credit that we care so much about other women's feelings. But not at the expense of making the right decision for ourselves. Instead of wasting our energy on guilt, let's work together toward actively supporting diverse choices, each and every one worthy of respect.

AFFIRMATION: Enough with the guilt.

*At fifty-two I've survived the long journey bridging my
mother-self to my apprentice crone self.*
                                    —HENRIETTA BENSUSSEN

It is both humbling and exciting to be near the end of one
stage and just taking our first baby steps toward the next.

As mothers we prided ourselves on our competence;
we've made the journey from novice to expert, having at-
tained "veteran status," skillful and sure of ourselves.

Now, once again, we find ourselves in the position of
apprentices, tentatively feeling our way toward this next
stage in our maturation process—as wise and knowing
crone. Once again we begin at the beginning.

AFFIRMATION: I am growing into my new self.

SUICIDAL THOUGHTS

When I was almost fifty with frequent and intense hot flashes, I sometimes had brief thoughts of suicide. And I mean brief.

—JEAN MOUNTAINGROVE

These words are important to heed, not as sensationalism or scare tactics but rather to acknowledge those of us who entertain brief—and I mean brief—thoughts of suicide.

Why does this occur during menopause? Physical symptoms can be so debilitating that we become severely depressed; in the extreme, we may fantasize about getting out of pain by ending our lives. The emotional trauma of midlife shifts can also cause serious despair.

Fleeting fantasies don't in themselves spell trouble. If however, they are ongoing, obsessive, or have reached the point of strategizing methods, it's time to act. Call a friend, a crisis-intervention hot line, or a counselor, spiritual leader, or medical provider. Do it right now.

AFFIRMATION: If I'm sinking, I need to seek help.

This health issue might receive a lot more attention if hot flashes happened to men.

—PAT MILLER

Might is putting it mildly. It reminds me of the quote "If men could get pregnant, abortion would be a sacrament."

We can safely assume that if hot flashes, vaginal dryness (switch the anatomy), osteoporosis, or any of the other physical aspects of menopause happened to men, they'd be right at the top of the Urgent Medical Research List, funded with serious money from major corporations, which are also, not coincidentally, run by men.

Which is all the more reason why it's important for women to lobby for medical research on bone-density loss, heart disease, breast cancer, and every other midlife medical issue. We must speak out, contributing our time, our energy, our finances to make midlife a priority, with the best minds and the best resources dedicated to our life-and-death concerns.

AFFIRMATION: Putting women's health care on the back burner has to stop. Here's how I'm willing to help:

God, the worst thing about this menopause stuff is that it requires me to be good to my body.

—PAT RHODA

We're challenged to eat well, exercise, and moderate our caffeine, sugar, nicotine, and alcohol use in order to maximize our health during menopause and midlife.

Sometimes it's a drag, especially on days when we're so stressed out, all we really want is beer and pretzels in front of the television.

Everything in moderation. As Dena Taylor, in her essay "Tofu and Tequila," writes, "I can't put just anything into my body without feeling its effects. So I decide whether it's worth it, and sometimes it is."

It's a good Rx for the fine balance of caring for ourselves without sacrificing too much.

AFFIRMATION: I can make small changes.

MONTH TEN **DAY FIVE**

Women who have careers feel the pressure not to disrupt their professional lives.

—CONNIE BATTEN

So many of us are already overworked, undernourished, and running on empty.

Now we have sleepless nights, hot flashes, and other menopausal ups and downs to disrupt our ability to function well in the workplace.

It's really hard to keep it all together. We don't want special dispensation, we certainly don't want to be seen as incompetent. By the same token, we *do* need that extra bit of support from employers and co-workers.

How do we get it? By explaining that we're under added stress while reaffirming our commitment. By seeking out co-workers who are in the same stage of life. And by reminding ourselves every day:

AFFIRMATION: I'm doing the best I can.

HOT FLASH: Cut back your schedule fifty
percent.
—LYDIA P.

A bit drastic (not to mention unrealistic) for most
of us, but for Lydia, a forty-seven-year-old retail
manager and mother of three, it was the only
way to compensate for feeling incredibly out of
whack in the first six months of her menopause.
"I went on part-time at work, I resigned from all
the committees I was on, and I hired a college
student to chauffeur my college kids to all their
activities so that I could get some rest," Lydia
says.

Drastic measures and the financial means to
carry them out made it possible for Lydia to dramatically reduce her responsibilities. Most of us
would happily settle for the lifting of a small frac-
tion of our pressures while we deal with menopausal symptoms: a little more help from our
spouse, fewer hours at work, more cooperation
from children so that we don't have to badger
them constantly to do their homework or
straighten up their rooms.

What matters is to look at our schedules, figure
out what's urgent and what's not, where it's possible to get some help, and then do what we can
to make it happen.

What can you do to reduce the pressure in your life? Are there areas in which you can compromise your perfectionism in order to give yourself a break? Can you relinquish, delegate, or abdicate any of your responsibilities? Can anything be put on hold? Is there any way to get more help and support?

It's easy to fall into a self-destructive pattern in which we take on too much and then feel resentful at the amount of responsibility we're carrying on our shoulders.

Stop a moment and think of one or two ways you can realistically cut back. What are they? Are you willing to take the first steps?

*So far, Day One, forty feels fine. The days of expensive
fashion errors, crazed momentary friendships and 2:00
A.M. feedings are over.*

—ANNA QUINDLEN

We breathe a sigh of relief as we realize all we have to
celebrate in turning forty: the impulsively purchased Mylar
miniskirt, now shoved into the back of our closet; the lost
souls we spent all night counseling in coffeehouses; the days
when the demands of early motherhood left us drained and
exhausted, fantasizing about Swiss boarding schools.

Each of us has our own list of ways in which forty—or
fifty—feels fine. Better than fine. At the top of *my* list goes
wearing a bikini in Jamaica without worrying whether anyone's noticing that my stomach sticks out. After that I'd add:
My daughter baby-sits for other children now instead of
needing a baby-sitter herself. Not being afraid of my parents
anymore. Having enough money to buy gourmet coffee
without counting pennies in a jar.

What's at the top of your list?

**AFFIRMATION: Now that I'm forty (or fifty), I'm
thankful for . . .**

> *The menopause is nature's original contraception to free women up for leadership.*
>
> —GERMAINE GREER

Makes sense. The majority of women in power (be they heads of corporations or heads of state) are typically women who've either remained child-free or older women who are unencumbered by the conflicting demands of career and motherhood.

In midlife we may find ourselves with the time, energy, and resources to finally burst into positions of power. The sad part is that we're often forced to wait too long, postponing high-level leadership roles until well into our fifties.

We need to work toward creating better support systems for women so that we can all pursue our dreams—motherhood, leadership, or any combination that frees us to move into center stage.

AFFIRMATION: I'm a born leader.

I am where I am because I believe in all possibilities.
—WHOOPI GOLDBERG

Which brings up yet one more important step to fulfilling our goals: Perhaps the single most essential element that comes before everything else is the ability to envision the future, with a firm belief that everything is possible.

Few of us are quite so optimistic. We tend to put road-blocks in our own path, coming up with countless (and often good) reasons to give up our goals. But as Whoopi Goldberg reminds us, having a vision, holding tightly to it, and believing in it with our hearts is the only way to combat cynicism. If we believe it is possible, we are more than halfway there.

AFFIRMATION: I believe.

A woman who does not wish to dump or deny a part of herself will not try to junk her used face.

—GERMAINE GREER

There are a couple of radical assumptions implicit in this statement: (a) that any woman who opts for cosmetic surgery is denying her aging and compromising her integrity; (b) that choosing to avail oneself of cosmetic surgery is self-hating, self-destructive, and self-mutilating.

I say stop the value judgments. Those of us who wish to avail ourselves of this technology have every right to improve our appearance without being accused of "junking" parts of ourselves we'd simply like to change.

And those of us for whom this would be untenable have every right to choose otherwise.

AFFIRMATION: I'll keep my criticism to myself.

> *In Rajasthan, India, women who have gone through menopause need no longer to stay in "purdah" (veiled and secluded) with the other women.*
> —SUSAN PERRY AND KATHERINE A. O'HANLON, M.D.

Ironically women in midlife often talk about just the opposite: the joys of time spent in the company of women.

Needless to say, one is a form of "imprisonment," the other a free choice. Indian women in midlife may or may not jump at the chance to hang out with other women after years of being denied their inalienable rights.

What is important is to have the choice. Many of us are seizing the opportunity to spend more time with women as we're reaching our forties and fifties.

As we mature, we find that sisterhood, whether it's meeting friends for lunch on a regular basis, attending all-women's retreats, joining a women's therapy group, or signing up for a drumming class with our best friend, nourishes us to the depths of our soul.

AFFIRMATION: I enjoy the company of women.

HOT FLASH: Women are where it's at.

—ELAYNE V.

This woman, age fifty, isn't a lesbian, although many women in midlife are turning to other women as primary partners, both emotionally and sexually.

What she means, and what women in their forties and fifties repeatedly say, is that spending time with other women is one of the most important sources of support and companionship as we age.

If this sounds like male-bashing, I'm sorry. Men and women have different—equally valuable— things to offer us. Most of us have spent the past twenty or thirty years devoting an enormous amount of energy to our relationships with men. Now, in this stage of our lives, we have something new and wonderful to gain from the company of women.

Who are the primary women in *your* life? Are you making sure to spend time with them? What do you get out of these relationships?

If you are already spending significant time in the company of women, keep up the commitment; it will surely continue to sustain you in numerous ways.

If you are women-deprived, write down whatever opportunities you see for connecting on a regular basis.

I can bring more female companionship into my life by . . .

The empty nest is not always an unhappy one.
—SUSAN PERRY AND KATHERINE A. O'HANLON, M.D.

On the contrary, lots of women with grown children savor the newfound delights of having our nest all to ourselves. In fact, as the authors of *Natural Menopause* say, "Recent studies show that many women find that emptying the nest is a liberating experience." My informal surveys back this up.

Nancy, age fifty-one, whose youngest daughter recently went away to college, says, "I've waited for this moment for years. I've turned her bedroom into an art studio." Anna, forty-eight, echoes her sentiments, saying, "Finally my husband and I can make love without worrying about kids in the other room." Beverly says she loves not worrying about what's for dinner or when the laundry needs to be done.

These are but a few of the rewards of reclaiming our home—sans children—filling it up in ways that make us gratefully say:

AFFIRMATION: There's nothing empty about it.

*You don't know how miserable it is. You don't know
what it's like to be sitting in a meeting of all men with
a four-hundred-dollar suit on and feel a flash coming
on.*

—Anonymous

Unfortunately many of us know just how miserable it can be,
although I'd certainly advise this woman to put away her
four-hundred-dollar suit for now and wear something she can
sweat through without running to the dry cleaner every
other day.

And here are two more tips: (a) Make sure you have
friends who are also in menopause (something that appears
lacking in this woman's life); and (b) if you can't stop feeling
angry, find a good therapist.

If this sounds harsh, consider the alternative: We can
nurse our anger and resentment until it eats away at our
insides and alienates others, or we can find a way of releasing
it so that we can start finding ways to cope productively with
the more "miserable" aspects of menopause.

AFFIRMATION: I don't have to suffer in silence.

MONTH TEN   **DAY SEVENTEEN**

*I refuse to admit that I'm 52, even if that does make
my sons illegitimate.*

—LADY MARY ASTOR

According to Miss Manners, my personal favorite arbiter of
"good taste," it's considered rude to ask a woman her age.

I say, "No way!" Let's make a radical change in how we
present ourselves to the world. Telling our age is something
to be proud of. "I'm fifty! Look how much I've accomplished!" "I'm seventy and I sure have seen a lot in my
lifetime!"

The next time someone asks your age, hesitate if you
must, then take a deep breath and proudly say,

AFFIRMATION: I'm_____and I'm proud of it.

Is it not strange that desire should so many years outlive performance?

—SHAKESPEARE

Shakespeare was talking about sex, which isn't surprising, given that typically men's libidos drop off significantly, affecting performance in midlife.

Women, in contrast, reach new peaks, which can create tension and frustration between us and our mates.

How do we handle this? First, by not taking our mate's lowered lust level personally. It is not a reflection of his love or attraction for us.

Second, we must have realistic expectations. And third, we can recommit to the art of self-pleasure. In these ways we can avoid letting natural differences in libido dictate the quality of our intimate relationship.

AFFIRMATION: I can satisfy myself.

Sooner or later the middle-aged woman becomes aware of a change in other people's attitudes toward her.
—GERMAINE GREER

Although this quote from Greer's book *The Invisible Change* doesn't explicitly define change as negative, it's safe to assume she's referring to ways in which middle-aged women are slighted, patronized, discounted, or ignored—all of which cuts to the core. Being treated as second-class citizens because we're over thirty-five is simply rude and shouldn't be tolerated.

Having made that clear, perhaps midlife women also generate some positive attitude changes; in some cases maturity may command greater respect. Our ideas may be taken more seriously; we're less intimidated and more of a presence to contend with.

Although we can't alter others' attitudes, we *can* take a hard look at our own biases against aging, making sure we're not buying into cultural stereotypes that cast a negative light on women in midlife.

AFFIRMATION: I am older and wiser, and I *will* be taken seriously.

HOT FLASH: Look at how you treat other
women.

—SONDRA M.

"I had no idea how often I put down older
women, until my friend Caron pointed it out to
me," confesses Sondra, a forty-six-year-old nutri-
tionist. "We were waiting in line behind this grand-
motherly-like type who was taking forever, and I
made some crack about giving her some adrenaline to get her going. Caron looked at me and
said, 'Watch it. That's you and me just a few years
from now.' "

How we treat other women is a statement of
how we feel about ourselves. Most of us struggle
with some degree of internalized oppression,
which we rid ourselves of by honestly examining
our negative biases.

It's time to examine our own prejudices, the negative stereotypes against aging that color our own attitude toward ourselves and other women in midlife.

What biases are *you* aware of that may consciously or subconsciously be at play? Here are a few examples: Youth is beauty. Older women are drab and unattractive. Women reach their prime in their thirties. Forty is the beginning of our decline.

As honestly as possible, try to identify your negative biases. State them in the following space:

1. _____
2. _____
3. _____

Remember, naming our prejudices is the first step toward transforming them into more positive images.

CLARITY

I'm having a midlife crisis, or should I say, a midlife clarity.

—KENNY LOGGINS

Increased clarity is yet another gift of midlife.

With time we are able to understand the significance of our life experiences. We see clearly where we've been. We identify the pivotal moments that shaped our identity, what they mean, and how to learn from them as we carry on.

And with enhanced clarity we gain wisdom. Gradually everything falls into place as we're able to put the pieces of our lives into perspective.

AFFIRMATION: I can see more clearly now.

All mothers weep for their children's childhood.
—GERMAINE GREER

As we put away the relics of our children's younger years, retiring their favorite stuffed animal to the attic, we become more acutely aware of our own aging.

Once, they required our constant attention; now, as often as not, they'd rather be with their friends. Once, they were small enough to cradle in our arms; now they tower over us, old enough for prom dresses, driver's licenses (gasp!), first jobs, falling in love, even permanent moves away from home.

As our children grow and go off, we may weep for the sweet, priceless time when they were, oh, so small. And we may leap with joy that they are growing or grown, gradually giving us back our lives. We are forever their mother but are also freer now to follow our dreams.

AFFIRMATION: Where has the time gone?

> *It is a bitter irony that most of the caring for aged parents has to be undertaken by their menopausal daughter.*
>
> —GAIL SHEEHY

Being the middle layer of the "sandwich generation"—caring for both growing children and aging parents—forces us to take on new responsibilities. In some ways the timing couldn't be worse. Right in the midst of menopause, when we're already struggling with exhaustion and upheaval, we're called upon to put aside our needs and do that much more!

So where does that leave us? Here are two suggestions for coping with aging parents at an inevitably inopportune time: (a) If you have siblings, *make sure* they're sharing the load; and (b) take extra good care of yourself, keeping in mind that:

AFFIRMATION: The more energy I put out, the more nurturing I need and deserve.

*A woman's life is a succession of lives, each revolving
around some emotionally compelling life experience.*
           —WALLIS SIMPSON, DUCHESS OF WINDSOR

At each pivotal stage we are emotionally challenged in
unique and different ways.

In adolescence we face intensely compelling physical and
emotional transformations as we begin the journey toward
womanhood. In pregnancy we face intensely compelling
physical and emotional transformations as we begin the journey toward motherhood.

Likewise, as we go through menopause, we face intensely
compelling emotional and physical changes as we begin the
journey toward our complete fulfillment as mature human
beings.

Indeed, we live many lives. Each new stage marks the end
of one passage and the beginning of the next.

**AFFIRMATION: I commit myself to fully experiencing
this new stage of life.**

Once women pass fifty, they may be able to tap into the feisty girls they once were.

—CAROLYN HEILBRUN

Contemporary feminist thinkers, particularly sociologist Carol Gilligan, believe that our feistiness is forced out of us by the time we reach early adolescence. That the boisterous, tree-climbing, trail-blazing, jubilant energy of girlhood is systematically subverted into passivity and compliance.

Apparently once we no longer feel so constrained by cultural female norms, so pressured to be nice girls, good mothers, understanding wives, we revert to our naturally rambunctious selves.

What a pity it takes this long! But we have lots of years left to make up for lost time. Start now. Let the feisty little girl inside you out. Get to know her again. Welcome her back into your life.

AFFIRMATION: There's no stopping me now!

HOT FLASH: Make waves.

—LYNN G.

"I spent the first forty-five years of my life worrying I'd be too loud, too brassy, too out there, but, boy, have I changed since turning fifty," says Lynn, a fifty-one-year-old attorney. "Now I say anything I want and let the chips fall where they may!"

The freedom to be ourselves, to be as "out there" as we feel like, is one great benefit of mid-life. We stop feeling intimidated, stop suppressing our feistiness, and are willing to make waves without worrying about what other people think.

Making waves doesn't make us insensitive. It simply means we're willing to put ourselves on the line.

Last night I caught actress Ellen Barkin, age forty-seven, on *Late Night with David Letterman.* I was struck by how well she "handled" the host. With a great deal of confidence and savvy, dressed in a mini-mini-mini-skirt, she ran the show, alternately sassy and dead serious, sometimes teasing, sometimes directly confrontational, leading David to point out how "feisty" she seemed.

Maybe *feisty* is just another word for freedom. In what ways are *you* becoming feistier and freer to express who you really, truly are?

*I would sit in a corner of my mind droning a mantra
that I'd conjured as self-defense: "Happiness is the best
face-lift. Happiness is the best face-lift. Happiness is the
best face-lift."*

—CATHLEEN ROUNTREE

It's probably true. Deep-down happiness radiates from the
inside out; we look younger, prettier, more vibrant when
we're feeling good.

Which doesn't mean we can—or should—will ourselves
to "put on a happy face." Forcing ourselves to defend
against the complexity of our real feelings tightens and tenses
us, achieving the opposite effect.

Sadness, when we allow ourselves to feel it without trying
to plaster on a smile, is also a natural beautifier. As is anger.
And grief.

Instead of saying, "Happiness is the best face-lift" consider this mantra:

**AFFIRMATION: Releasing all my feelings is the only
path to peace.**

> *Nobody in Hollywood says, "Oh, boy—let's do a play about a fifty-five-year-old woman who falls in love."*
> —Wendy Wasserstein

So many of us are finding romance in our forties and fifties through love affairs, second marriages, or the occasional fling. Love *doesn't* happen just to ingenues, contrary to what Hollywood would have us believe. We're hungry for images of midlife women, turned on by love, as evidenced by the runaway success of the novel *The Bridges of Madison County,* whose story line is based on a forty-four-year-old woman who finds herself in an unexpected romantic encounter.

So, Wendy, I guess it's up to you. Or me. Whether it's cinema roles, music lyrics, or characters in novels, *we,* as women, must put our creative energy into making films, music, and books starring women in midlife falling in love *and* making it work.

AFFIRMATION: Every day is an opportunity to fall in love.

How old would you be if you didn't know how old you are?

—SATCHEL PAIGE

Most of us are limited by preconceived ideas about age. Whether or not we're consciously aware of it, we may sabotage ourselves by believing that age forty or fifty, by definition, constricts our capacities in ways that keep us from being all we can be.

But ask yourself this: How old would you be if there were no birthdays, no calendar years to dictate how you feel inside? Does your energy level defy the wrinkles you see in the mirror? Do you feel like a teenager? An old soul? Exactly your age?

AFFIRMATION: I feel _____ years old.

COMMITMENT

How we spend our days is how we spend our years.
                                        —ANNIE DILLARD

As we round the midpoint of our lives, we may say to ourselves, *I had better make good use of my remaining years.*

But as writer Annie Dillard points out, how we spend our days *is* how we spend our years. How we fill every single day —today, tomorrow, and the next—what impact we make, what work we produce, what people we touch ultimately decides the value of our lives.

As we get older, we become more conscious of how we spend each day, making sure we are giving and getting as much as we can.

How did *you* spend today? How will you spend tomorrow?

AFFIRMATION: Tomorrow I will . . .

Solitude has become very important to me. That seems to come with the fifties.

—ELLEN BURSTYN

As each year passes, we become more protective of our solitude; we treasure the bliss of uninterrupted hours to read, write, and dream, to do anything *we* feel like in the blessed time and space we carve out for ourselves.

We prize time alone far more than we did in our twenties or thirties. We're no longer afraid of being alone; we feel confident of our ability to gather friends when we're feeling social and be alone when that's what we crave.

Knowing how to be alone is an art that comes with age. Enjoying our own company frees us to choose companionship or solitude, with confidence that:

AFFIRMATION: I'm fine either way.

LETTING GO

Grown don't mean nothing to a mother.
—TONI MORRISON

In our midyears those of us who are mothers are challenged to let go of our children, which is one of the most painful, difficult, and necessary aspects of parenting.

It's hard to stop telling our children how to live their lives, even when they're old enough to date, drive cars, hold jobs, and live away from home. It's hard to watch them make mistakes; whether they're five years old or twenty-five years old, they're still our babies, and we'd do anything to prevent their being hurt.

But we can't. The older we get—and the older they get —the more we need to respect their judgment, offering wisdom when asked, trusting that:

AFFIRMATION: I've given my children the tools, now it's up to them to live their own lives.

*I put myself ahead twenty years and try to look at what
I need to do now in order to get there then.*

—DIANA ROSS

This quote from Diana Ross's autobiography offers sound
advice for being active architects in designing the next decades of our lives.

Having goals is just the first step: "I want to be retired by
the time my children are grown." "I plan to spend my
fiftieth birthday in Paris." "I intend to complete writing a
novel before I turn sixty."

Reaching our goals requires some commitment and planning: "I will start an IRA that will mature the year my son
graduates high school." "I will take French classes and start
a special travel savings account." "I will put aside every
Saturday afternoon to write, even if it takes the next twenty
years."

We get there by setting our goals and starting on the path
toward reaching them, step by step, beginning today.

AFFIRMATION: Ten years from now I intend to . . .

HOT FLASH: Make a map for how you
want to spend the next ten or twenty years.
—JENNIFER H.

Jennifer, forty-two, a nurse who paints in her
spare time, has mapped out the next eight years
of her life: "I've decided that by age fifty I want to
have the freedom to paint full-time, and the only
way to ensure that is by working double shifts at
the hospital and forgoing vacations until I have
enough money to devote myself to my art." In
addition Jennifer has joined a women's support
group where she gets "constant support to keep
up the hard work."

   Some of us are very clear about our goals,
some of us are still cloudy, and some of us prefer
to take a more flexible, let's-see-what-comes-next
attitude toward the future. Whatever our personal
style, what matters is to know that we have the
power to get where we want to go.

Mapping out our lives involves three distinct steps:

1. Identifying our goals
2. Figuring out how to reach them
3. Making the commitment to do what it takes

Contemplate where you want to be in the next five, ten, and twenty years. Then complete the following sentences:

1. My five-year goal is to . . .
2. I will get there by . . .
3. I am ready to make the commitment to . . .

Now do the same exercise, only this time based on where you'd like to see yourself in ten years, fifteen years, and twenty years.

SECURITY

> *There are those of us who think settled is synonymous*
> *with death and stagnation; I'm the kind who thinks*
> *settled is synonymous with security.*
>
> —ANNA QUINDLEN

The word *settled* has come to have negative connotations;
what comes to mind is a middle-aged person who's given up
her dreams and settled into a boring, complacent, altogether
predictable existence.

But as writer Anna Quindlen points out, being settled can
also mean being peaceful, secure, comfortable with who we
are and what we've made of our lives.

Hopefully in our midyears we are as alive as ever. And
hopefully we enjoy the comfort that comes of having settled
some of the big questions: with whom we are living our
lives, our career path, our values and goals, so that we can sit
back and relax.

**AFFIRMATION: I'm not stagnating. I'm comfortable
and secure.**

*In traditional Judaism a girl's first menstrual period is
acknowledged by a slap in the face instantly followed by
a piece of candy.*

—FOLKLORE

This tradition is part of Jewish cultural folklore, although
I've never met a mother who actually celebrated her daughter's first period this way. And as I anticipate my daughter,
Zoe's, imminent passage into adolescence, I seriously question the wisdom, although the candy part sounds okay.

Still, the symbolism isn't lost on me. The onset of menstruation—just as the onset of menopause—*is* a significant
emotional slap in the face, a mixed bag of sadness and joy,
sorrow and anticipation. Both life passages are at once sobering and sweet; both require us to stop and say to ourselves:

AFFIRMATION: This is a bittersweet moment.

ADVENTURE

> *On my 50th birthday, after just three skiing lessons, I*
> *went to the tallest mountain in Vail, Colorado, and*
> *skiied down.*
>
> —CHARLAYNE HUNTER-GAULT

Good for you! And good for any of us who celebrate birthday milestones in a spectacular way!

One woman, Maja, plans to spend her fortieth birthday in Bali; she says, "I've decided I want to be somewhere as far away and different as I can find." Another, Emily, went on an archeological dig in Egypt; still another, Sara, spent the entire day of her fortieth birthday in bed—a radical departure from her usual hectic schedule.

But we needn't wait for birthdays to do something new or exciting. We can start today. It needn't be spectacular, just off the beaten track from your normal routine. You'll be amazed at how rejuvenated you'll feel.

AFFIRMATION: I think I'll try . . .

MONTH ELEVEN   **DAY ELEVEN**

*When I was thirty I didn't work out at all. Now, if a
day goes by and I don't work out I feel badly.*
                                        —RUTH ZAPORAH

Wow! If I manage to make it to the health club twice a
month, I'm doing great!

There's no question—the older we get, the more our
bodies need strong, regular workouts to stay in shape. For
some of us this might mean a daily, no-excuses-unless-I'm-
dying regime; exercising once or twice a week also makes a
difference in our energy and attitude.

Whether we're workout junkies or once-a-weekers,
there's no point in feeling guilty about what we're *not* doing.
Effort is everything. If you miss today, try again tomorrow.

AFFIRMATION: I feel good about the exercise I get.

We try to live our hundred days in one; get all the feelings, bend all the notes.

—BILLIE HOLIDAY

"And you can't do all you want to in the time you've got," blues singer Billie Holiday wisely says.

We can, however, make sure we get everything out of the time that remains.

Whereas once it seemed as if we had our whole lives ahead of us, now we become more aware of the finite nature of time. In our forties and fifties we come to grips with the reality that we aren't going to be able to do everything, making it all that imperative to do what's truly essential to our being.

We needn't feel panicky about time passing. Rather we can see it as an opportunity to redefine our personal commitments, making sure to make every day count.

AFFIRMATION: I'm giving it my all.

HOT FLASH: Get your priorities straight.
                              —ALLISON E.

"Since turning fifty, I've made myself a promise to stop wasting my time on *anything* that isn't an absolute priority," says Allison, a lobbyist. "I've figured out that the three most important things are my health, my children, and my career. Anything else takes a backseat."

How does this play out in Allison's life? As she explains, "I work out three times a week, no matter what. I devote as much time as I can to the kids, even if it means sacrificing friendships. And I don't do any volunteer work that will skim off the energy I need to put in eight-to-ten-hour days at the legislature."

Our priorities will continue to shift. But knowing what matters most—right now—is the best way to get the most out of every day.

Are *your* priorities in order, or are you squandering valuable time and energy on things that aren't essential to your happiness and well-being?

Here's one way to find out. List your three most important commitments, in order of their significance:

1. _____
2. _____
3. _____

Now consider a typical day in your life. How closely does your daily schedule reflect your priorities?

We should get medals for having survived considering what women have to go through to reach the age of fifty-five.

—GLORIA ALLARD

Gold medals, that is! Trophies for all the challenges met, obstacles triumphed over, personal struggles transcended in the course of forty or fifty years.

Each of has made Olympian efforts; each of us is a champion in the truest sense of the word.

Consider for a moment the "marathons" you've run— and won—in order to have reached this point. You might include some of the following: Childbirth and mothering. Relationships. Career successes, along with the adversities you've faced and survived along the way.

We may never have a gold medal to place on our mantel. Which makes it that much more important to say to ourselves:

AFFIRMATION: I've been through so much and I've handled it like a champion.

VISUALIZATION

Legend tells of the woman who would frequently stick her head into the freezer to cool off.

—PAT MILLER

It's worth imagining.

Many women in menopause swear by mental imagery and other visualization techniques as a way of countering the effects of hot flashes and other physical discomforts.

Here's how it works: The next time you experience a hot flash or any other symptoms, take a moment to close your eyes. Find a comfortable position. Notice your breathing. Allow the breath to wash in and out of you. Now, in your mind's eye, imagine a freezing ice cube rubbed over your entire body to cool you off. Imagine a beautiful flower to remind you of your connection to nature. Imagine a gentle rainstorm to comfort and soothe you. Allow yourself to drift and dream. Allow your imagination to alter your experience.

AFFIRMATION: Visualization is a powerful healing tool.

MONTH ELEVEN   **DAY SEVENTEEN**

I am now grateful for the "Have you enclosed your check?" reminder.

—GAYLE SAND

We joke about early Alzheimer's, about forgetting where we're going or finding our car keys in the freezer. But in fact, for many women memory loss or lapses is a serious psychological and physiological part of menopause.

It doesn't mean we're going crazy or losing our mind. It *does* mean we need to honestly face any memory loss we're aware of, let our medical provider know, and do whatever we can to accommodate it.

It's natural to feel embarrassed or worried about memory loss. It's critical to speak up and get support.

AFFIRMATION: Now, what was I saying?

Someone once said, "You have the menopause you de-
serve."

—ISABEL ALLENDE

This quote can easily be misinterpreted as meaning that the difficult symptoms of menopause are our own fault, our responsibility, our karma or repayment for having in some way screwed up.

Here's a different, more positive interpretation: We get the menopause we *need.* Our hot flashes, headaches or heartaches are gifts, celestial nudges to slow down, improve our diet, get more exercise, more leisure time, more emotional support.

Perhaps, in both a practical and a cosmic sense, getting what we deserve simply means doing everything we can to take advantage of how menopause motivates us to make changes for the better.

AFFIRMATION: I'm open to the possibilities.

She feared she was really crazy, she spent so much of her time angry.

—DORIS LESSING

The worst thing about anger is how frightened it makes us feel. Our impatience, mood swings, and angry outbursts make us wonder if we're losing it—if menopause has robbed us of our ability to control ourselves and keep a reasonable check on our emotions.

If this sounds like you, the first thing to know is *you're not crazy*. Anger is a natural and appropriate response to menopausal symptoms that are affecting the quality of your life.

However, this doesn't give us license to act out and lash out. Being abusive isn't the answer; in fact it's a sign we need to seek help. Finding ways of releasing anger constructively —whether through professional counseling, a support group, or doing karate chops in your basement—will help you get a handle on your emotions.

AFFIRMATION: I will find appropriate ways of expressing my anger.

HOT FLASH: Let it all out.

—PAULA B.

"Quit pretending to yourself and everyone else that everything's okay," says Paula, "and just be as angry as you really are."

For Paula, who's spent the past three years struggling with hourly hot flashes, letting out anger was a necessary part of coming to grips with her understandable frustration.

Expressing what you are feeling rather than putting on an act is good advice, especially for women. We've been taught to control anger instead of expressing it. However, there's a difference between destructive and constructive anger, between letting other people have it and letting our feelings out in a healthy and responsible way.

It's up to us to find ways of venting our anger without taking it out on anyone else.

Few of us are anger-free, especially when it comes to coping with the more difficult aspects of menopause.

Naming and releasing our feelings is a healthy, constructive way of getting anger out. It may not "solve" our problems, but you'd be amazed at how much it helps just to say:

I'm angry about . . .
Here's how I really feel: . . .

Releasing anger, whether we whine with our friends, write in our journals, or throw a fit in the safety of a therapist's office, is a necessary part of maintaining mental health.

We deserve the right to be angry—so long as we're willing to take an active role in our own healing.

AUTHENTICITY

Turning into my own / turning on into my own self at last.

—LUCILLE CLIFTON

These words from poet Lucille Clifton beautifully describe the growing authenticity we feel as we move into our mid-years.

At last we are turning into our own person. At last we are turning on to all the beauty we contain, especially once we stop censoring parts of ourselves and step fully into our own power and light.

In the words of the famous educator Marva Collins, "Imitation is suicide." The older we are, the less we imitate others, be it our mothers, our teachers, or any other role models we've emulated. Instead we are at long last liberated to be absolutely true to ourselves.

AFFIRMATION: My real self continues to emerge.

I've got to steal some time for myself.

—LEONTYNE PRICE

We are always stealing time for ourselves, feeling slightly guilty about it, like children copping a cookie from the cookie jar, afraid of getting caught. We're nervous and apologetic. "I just *had* to get away for an hour," we mutter defensively. "I've waited for a vacation for ten years," we explain.

But we have nothing to explain or apologize for. We needn't think of it as "stealing time" but rather "taking time," a difference that goes beyond verbal semantics. We're helping ourselves to what is rightfully ours.

AFFIRMATION: I have the right to take time for myself.

SELF-ACTUALIZATION

I am a self-made woman.

—SOJOURNER TRUTH

These words were written in 1882 by one of the earliest feminists and abolitionists, Sojourner Truth.

It is an equally powerful affirmation for women today. We must claim the ways in which we are responsible for our growth and development: "I have learned how to be a good mother through trial and error." "I have worked hard for the worldly success I've achieved." "I have spent years in therapy healing my pain and remaking myself into a healthier, more competent human being."

None of it happens without effort. We can—and must—congratulate ourselves for all the hard work.

AFFIRMATION: I am a self-made woman.

We need to begin treating ourselves as well as we treat other people. That would be an enormous revolution!
—GLORIA STEINEM

Amen! Over and over we hear doomsday rumblings over the imminent demise of the women's movement.

But what a revolution it would be if we, as women, started treating ourselves with the care, respect, and attention we devote to others. What a radical transformation to offer ourselves the level of care, compassion, acceptance, and support we routinely give.

Here is another midlife opportunity for growth. Think about what would happen if we treated ourselves as well as we treat our best friend, beloved child, or cherished mate. Imagine how much stronger and happier we'd be!

AFFIRMATION: Start the revolution!

I started body surfing in my fifties!

—COLEEN KEIBUS

Add this to your list of Wonderful Things I'm Going to Do the Day I Turn Fifty.

But why wait? There's no minimum age requirement for trying new and exciting adventures. Today's as good a day as any to start body surfing. To get your pilot's license or buy a camcorder and become an amateur film producer or any of endless other ways to add a little thrill to our lives.

Pick out one activity you've put on hold until you turn forty or fifty or sixty that you're willing to get started on now. Are you ready?

AFFIRMATION: Yes. Today I will try . . .

HOT FLASH: Don't let your fear get in your way.

—MAB NULTY

In her forty-first year my dear friend Mab decided to do something she'd always dreamed of. "I wanted to swim with the dolphins," she says, "so we planned a trip to the Florida Keys, and I actually did it!"

For Mab swimming with the dolphins required breaking through a substantial amount of fear. "I'm not that great a swimmer, scuba diving terrifies me, but I was determined to have this experience no matter what it took."

Breaking through fear is exhilarating and deeply rewarding. We discover what we're made of. In the process we free ourselves to experience adventures we'd never thought possible.

Pushing through our fear allows us more fully to experience life.

How is fear getting in the way of challenges, activities, or adventures you'd like to have? What are you willing to do about it?

Complete the following sentence:

The one thing I'm dying to do but am scared of is . . .

Next complete this sentence:

If I do this, the worst thing that can happen is . . .

Now ask yourself, am I willing to take the risk?

If the answer is no, return to this exercise six months or a year from now. If the answer is yes, then complete this final sentence:

I will pursue this adventure by the time I'm . . .

Now move on to the next quote, which hopefully will fortify you on the road to adventure.

*That's one of the good things about being fifty. You're
no longer so easily scared.*

—ISABEL ALLENDE

Which helps put risk taking into perspective.

As we reach midlife, we're far more able to make decisions, take risks, try new things without being crippled by the fear of failure—or the equally intimidating possibility of success.

Whether it's getting a dramatically different hairstyle, changing our vocation, or entering a new intimate relationship, we're less scared of the unknown, more confident in our capacity to come through.

With time and experience we have faith that:

AFFIRMATION: No matter what comes, I have what it takes to handle it.

We have brains. We are beautiful. We can do anything we set our minds to.

—DIANA ROSS

I'm tempted to copy this and put it next to my bed. There are days when I (and all of us) feel anything *but* intelligent, beautiful, and able to conquer the world.

But we are. And we can.

It helps to be reminded of this every now and then. And it helps to notice how much more often we believe it now, in our forties and fifties, than we did in our twenties and thirties.

Seeing ourselves as intelligent, beautiful, capable beings is an ongoing process. We are unlikely to maintain this degree of confidence on a daily basis. (Even Diana has her bad days!) But chances are, with each day we get a little closer and more able to say:

AFFIRMATION: I'm intelligent. I'm beautiful. I can do anything I set my mind to.

We do not know why it happens.

—GERMAINE GREER

This simple truth—number two on Greer's lengthy list entitled "What We Don't Know About Menopause"—is particularly intriguing.

Expectant mothers deal with a similarly confounding and mysterious experience of not knowing what makes labor contractions begin. It's aggravating because we can't conveniently time our childbirth, yet exciting as well, one of the few mysteries modern science has yet to crack.

Likewise we are somewhat in the dark when it comes to menopause. We know *what* occurs but are perplexed as to *why* it occurs, which leaves it to the imagination. Maybe menopause happens in order to give us a much-needed reprieve from menstruation. Maybe it happens to protect women in their midyears from the exhausting demands of motherhood (although this is one area where science is making inroads, implanting fetuses in fifty-year-old women). Perhaps it's nature's way of creating just enough turmoil to push us toward new breakthroughs in our spiritual journey.

What do you think?

AFFIRMATION: Maybe menopause occurs because . . .

OVERDOING

> *I've just taken belly dancing classes, a water color class,*
> *a doll making class.*
>
> —SUMASHIL

We get credit—and extra credit—every time we further our education, taking classes and seminars; going off on a renewal retreat; pursuing gourmet cooking, Rollerblading, or yoga.

But we can also go too far. We may overload our schedule and exhaust ourselves by pushing too hard, expecting too much, being too perfectionistic in our efforts to excel.

While midlife increases our inner urgency to educate and enrich ourselves, we needn't overreact by thinking time's running out.

It's not. Find the right balance between broadening your horizons and burning yourself out.

AFFIRMATION: I will pace myself.

MONTH TWELVE   **DAY THREE**

*Now that I'm almost fifty, I'm discovering that maybe I
don't have to have a man.*

—TABIA TUNOA

My twelve-year-old daughter use to play board games, build
obstacle courses, and bike-ride with her friends. Now they
spend hours either talking about boys, talking on the phone
to boys, or talking about who's been talking to which boy
about what on the phone. Their every moment is consumed
with gossip about who's going with whom and who's breaking up with whom, as if boys are the sole purpose of their
existence.

For them, for now, it is. In contrast, for those of us who
are, thankfully, years removed from the boy-crazy stage, it's
a great relief to know we can live just fine with or without a
man. Having a lover or mate can enhance our lives, but it's
no longer critical to our happiness.

**AFFIRMATION: I can choose to be with or without a
man.**

Leeches were often put on a woman's ears or the nape of her neck to cure menopausal complaints.
— SUSAN PERRY AND KATHERINE A. O'HANLON, M.D.

If leeches were once considered acceptable medical treatment for menopause, maybe we *have* come a long way, after all!

Of course it's all relative. Some less-than-satisfied customers of HRT are quick to describe their own version of medical horror stories. Says one woman, "Estrogen made me feel so sick and out of it, it may as well have been leeches for all the good it did."

We can be grateful for how far we've come *(anything's better than leeches!)* while still devoting our time, energy, money, and collective political clout to finding improved medical techniques for treating the symptoms of menopause.

AFFIRMATION: I appreciate the progress.

I think the middle years are a wonderful opportunity for women to see if they've yet figured out who they are.
—BROOKE MEDICINE EAGLE

Figuring out "who we are" is an ongoing process of discovery.

We know more about ourselves—what makes us tick, what truly fulfills us—as we come into our forties and fifties. Sometimes we're taken by surprise: After years of seeing myself as someone who couldn't make macaroni and cheese without burning it, I've suddenly realized I love to cook and am capable of whipping up an impressive gourmet meal when I set my mind to it.

Other aspects of our identity simply become clearer, more delineated with age: I've been writing down my thoughts in one form or another since I was eight.

Seeing "who we are" may come in the form of revelations or reinforcement for what we've long known. Both are gifts. Both demand our attention in our journey toward self-discovery.

AFFIRMATION: I keep figuring out more about myself.

HOT FLASH: Be open to change.

—NICOLE S.

At age fifty-two Nicole made a dramatic change in her life. "After spending most of my adult years working in the counseling field, I realized I wanted to do something more concrete, something that took muscle and sweat instead of intellectual and analytical skills."

Giving up her counseling practice and training to be a masseuse required Nicole to make two important shifts. First, she had to entertain a new and different image of herself. Second, she had to be willing to trade a lifetime of security for the unforeseen challenges ahead.

In other words she was open to change *and* willing to act on it.

Being receptive to new aspects of ourselves needn't necessitate such sweeping life changes. What matters is to be conscious of whether or not our choices continue to accurately reflect who we are today.

What new revelations about yourself have you experienced in the past year? Have you discovered that you love to dance? That you need greater stretches of solitude? That you're driven to work with the homeless in your community?
  Complete the following sentence:

  I have recently discovered that . . .

  Now ask yourself, What changes am I willing to make as a result of what I've learned about myself?

> *To me, the term "sexual freedom" meant freedom from*
> *having to have sex. And then along came Good Vibra-*
> *tions. Now I am a regular Cat on a Hot Tin Roof.*
>   —Lily Tomlin and Jane Wagner

One final word on vibrators and other sexual aids that may
be the answer—or at least part of the answer—for those of
us struggling with sexual frustration during menopause.

It's not for everybody. But many, many women agree that
a vibrator—whether used solo or in partnership with lovemaking—can enhance desire and increase sexual pleasure.

Having a vibrator by your bedside doesn't mean there's
anything wrong with you or your sexual relationship. On the
contrary it's a way of affirming your right to a more satisfying erotic experience. As Lily Tomlin's character, Judith
Beasely, in *The Search for Signs of Intelligent Life on the Planet*,
puts it, "Think of it as Hamburger Helper for the boudoir."

AFFIRMATION: I will give myself pleasure.

If a woman misses three periods, she is old, but if her period returns, she becomes young again.

—THE TALMUD

If HRT is part of our menopausal medical plan, we may find our periods stopping, then reappearing.

One day we feel as if we're truly in the Change, then our flow resumes, sometimes in the extreme, cramps and all, reminiscent of periods we had when we were fourteen and carried notes from our mother to get us out of gym.

Menstrual flow, whether caused by ovulation or estrogen, is no signifier of youth or maturity. Blood or no blood has little to do with how young or old we truly are. *Period.*

AFFIRMATION: My flow doesn't determine my youth or maturity.

MEANING

I used to trouble a lot about what life was for; now being alive seems sufficient reason.

—JOANNE FIELD

When my husband, Joey, turned forty-three, I asked him if he wished he could turn back the clock and be twenty-five again.

''Yes,'' he said, ''because if I had it all to do over again, I wouldn't agonize about the meaning of life, I'd just enjoy it.''

In our forties and fifties we have a pretty good idea of who we are and why we're here on earth. We're freer to live each day without constant existential crises, without analyzing everything to the nth degree.

We may never fully understand the meaning of life. Perhaps we're not meant to. Perhaps the real point is to appreciate and enjoy it.

AFFIRMATION: The meaning of life is a mystery. The purpose of life is to enjoy being alive.

MONTH TWELVE   DAY ELEVEN

My mind and body are going in the same direction, but not at the same speed.

—MARGARET RANDALL

As we mature, our intellect sharpens, our wisdom deepens, our vision expands. Simultaneously our bodies slow down, creating a gap between our ambition and our energy.

Once, we could stay up half the night passionately immersed in finishing a project; now we're dependent on eight hours of sleep. We used to be able to run three miles, put in a long day's work at the office, chase after toddlers, and still get around to vacuuming; now we need to take regular breaks and even then some of our to-do list doesn't get done.

That's okay. Midlife requires us to reconcile the scope of our goals with the limitations of our energy. We might not be able to do five things at once, but we *can* do one thing at a time and do it really, really well.

AFFIRMATION: I'm willing to trade quantity for quality.

Memories are our doors of escape, our compensation.
—DOROTHY DIX

It's one of the sweetest gifts of growing older: with each passing year we have more to reflect on, rich and colorful memories captured in photographs, and images and experiences stored in the scrapbook of our mind.

We stare at our high-school graduation picture, searching for glimmers of what we now see when we look in the mirror. Recollections of our thirtieth birthday party help us decide how we want to spend our fiftieth. Reveries of the fabulous two weeks we spent in Europe melt into memories of the terrifying ordeal when our youngest fell out of the tree, in cinema verité of the good times and the bad times. Together they paint a true picture of how we've lived our lives.

AFFIRMATION: My memories are a doorway into enlightenment.

HOT FLASH: Put your photographs in a scrapbook.

—JAN V.

That's how Jan spent her forty-fifth birthday. "I went through piles of all my old pictures and carefully put them into a hardcover album. Somehow it seemed urgent to get them out of the drawers and into a permanent collection."

It's one way to "preserve your memories," a poignant line from Simon and Garfunkel's early album *Bookends*. Collecting our photographs and putting them in a safe place helps us to reflect on our history and respect where we've been.

Have you taken the time to look through your old photographs? Are they floating around in the bottom of your drawers or are they carefully ensconced in a safe place where you will have them forever?

If you haven't yet, collecting your memories is a wonderful midlife project. Put your dried flowers, faded photographs, and other memorabilia in a special box or personal photo album so that you always have access to the significant moments in your past.

It is the fight itself that keeps you going.

—COLETTE

I assume writer Colette meant the word *fight* in the most positive sense—not as embattlement but rather as the energy, passion, and drive that motivates us in midlife.

For many of us the "fight" takes on a less desperate and combative edge; we're softer in our approach, yet no less adamant about winning our personal crusades, be they abortion rights, homelessness, improving education, or getting our husband to pick up his socks.

What are *you* fighting for? What issues inspire and keep you going?

AFFIRMATION: I care deeply about . . .

You should always know when you're shifting gears in life.

—LEONTYNE PRICE

In retrospect we can more easily see the significant passages in our lives. We review the meaningful markers: the birth of our children, the day we quit our job, holding our breath and having faith that we were on to something better, the Christmas we landed in the hospital with pneumonia and realized we'd come to an important crossroads and committed ourselves to pursuing much better self-care.

Midlife is yet another passage in which we are forced (or invited, depending on how we look at it) to shift gears. We may slow down or speed up. We may back up and reevaluate our road plan or we may grab our compass and head in a whole new direction.

How are *you* shifting gears right now? What physical, emotional, and spiritual adjustments are you making as a result of having reached this crossroads?

AFFIRMATION: I'm aware that I have reached a crossroads.

Now that I am fifty-six, come and celebrate with me!
—MURIEL RUKEYSER

These words are infused with exhilaration, gratitude, and joy.

Now that I am fifty-six: A moment worth waiting for, destination reached, journey completed.

Come and celebrate with me: An invitation—to ourselves and our loved ones—to mark midlife with gusto, perhaps festively throwing a party with fifty-six balloons.

What's more, poet Muriel Rukeyser isn't talking only about "milestone birthdays"—our fortieth or fiftieth—but her fifty-sixth, as if each year is equally worthy of celebration.

How will you spend your next birthday? Whom will you invite to share in the joy?

AFFIRMATION: Now that I am_____, come and celebrate with me.

GRATITUDE

This is the place of the breakthrough into abundance.
—Joseph Campbell

Women—and men, too, who are happy and fulfilled seem to share one important quality—*gratitude.* We're more aware of what we have than what we're missing. We count our blessings. We're less motivated by fear and more firmly rooted in our deep sense of abundance.

In other words, the cup is half full, and in some cases overflowing.

Cultivating an attitude of abundance doesn't mean burying our head in the sand, but rather being genuinely appreciative. In our midyears we give thanks for so very much: For our family and friends' health and happiness. For meaningful work. For the opportunity to have traveled. For the vast range of experiences we've been fortunate to have.

Take a moment now to be aware of the abundance in your life. Stop and offer thanks for all you've been given.

AFFIRMATION: I am breaking through into abundance.

Often continuity is visible only in retrospect.
—MARY CATHERINE BATESON

It's hard to see the continuity—the common threads and guiding principles—that have been constant through the various seasons of our lives.

When we look back, patterns emerge. We see how a decision made at twenty-one to change our major from biology to psychology led us to our present career. How all our primary love affairs have been with men we needed to take care of—and why. How our definition of a "good friend" is not different than it was when we were a teenager.

Identifying the lines of continuity helps us to understand how the woman we are right now is a natural extension of who we were at fifteen, twenty-five, and thirty-five.

AFFIRMATION: I am in a continual process of evolution.

HOT FLASH: Unravel the common threads
in your life.

—KATHLEEN R.

"I went to a women's retreat, and while we were
there, we did the Lifeline Exercise, in which we
plotted a graph of the most significant moments
of each decade," says Kathleen. "I was amazed
at the consistent themes that appeared over and
over again. For one thing I saw how every major
decision I'd made had to do with my inner struggle between dependence and independence.
For another I saw that the same issues I am dealing with in my second marriage are similar to
those I dealt with in my earliest relationships with
men."

Unraveling the common threads—the healthy
patterns as well as the lessons we continue to
learn and relearn—gives meaning to the past as
well as giving us insight for the future.

Here's how the Lifeline Exercise works:

1. Draw a straight line on a piece of paper that represents your life, demarking each decade.

2. Now fill in the most significant moments—positive and negative—of each decade. For example you might include your first romance, leaving home, starting college, getting married, having children, career changes, and any other personal epiphanies that have profoundly affected your life.

3. Once you've filled in your Lifeline, notice what these experiences have in common. See if you can discover the threads of continuity.

We seemed to be crafting lives we wanted rather than simply coping with the lives we had.

—JOANNA F. LACKER

In our midyears we also make the shift from merely living our lives to actively participating in their design. From coping to crafting, from handling our daily demands to having a firm hand in the creation of our future.

What does it mean to be architects of our own lives? It means seriously evaluating how to manifest our values. It means setting intentional goals and committing ourselves to reaching them. It means figuring out that this is *our* life; that rather than letting it happen we will *make* it happen, by taking full responsibility for realizing our dreams.

AFFIRMATION: I am crafting the life I want.

*I'm probably a better teacher than I would have been in
my twenties.*

—SHARON LESTER

No doubt! I'm certainly a better writer than I was in my
twenties. Not to mention a better mother. And for that
matter, wife.

Mastery grows with time. Our inevitable mistakes guide
us as we go; we're more confident, more knowledgeable,
more perceptive. Our experience can't help but make us
better able to excel at whatever we do.

Choose one or two areas in your life and take note of your
progress. Are you a better friend than you were five years
ago? A more seasoned artist? A more loving partner in your
intimate relationships?

AFFIRMATION: I'm definitely better at . . .

It took me a long way to get to where I am now.
—VIRGINIA MARINO

Which has a great deal to do with the mastery we've achieved.

It *has* taken a long time to reach this point. We've spent years developing our talents and skills, decades coming to a deeper understanding of ourselves. We've invested great sums of energy, hope, and heartache making the journey from student to teacher, from girlhood to womanhood.

We didn't just wake up at forty or fifty with all the grace and strength and power we have today. We earned it. And we can count on it to carry us through.

AFFIRMATION: I've made it.

My whole life I've been doing things for other people.
—PEG CURRAN

All the more reason why it's essential—make that *urgent*—to begin doing things for ourselves.

We take great pride in helping our spouses, our children, our parents, friends, and community.

But in midlife we must also seize the opportunity to turn some of our love and generosity inward.

It's easier said than done. After a lifetime of self-denial, we may not even know where to start.

Here's the way: For the next month make yourself this promise—every time I give something to someone else I will invest equal energy in doing something nice for myself.

Increase your tolerance for acts of kindness directed inward. Notice how good it feels to take as well as to give.

AFFIRMATION: It's my turn to receive.

SELF-RESPECT

Anybody who has been a homemaker needs to know she has value.

—PEG CURRAN

It used to be called the empty-nest syndrome; women who'd devoted years to raising a family and running a home faced emptiness and insecurity upon reaching middle age.

For those of us with careers, this might be an outdated, even irrelevant issue. But the fact remains, many women still find themselves in their forties or fifties unsure of their value, shaky about their marketable skills, scared about having to forge a new identity, particularly if it means finding well-paying work.

First, we must find self-respect. We must consciously take stock of all the skills, knowledge, and capabilities we've gained in the process of being a mother and homemaker. *We must take pride in how we've spent our years, placing value on having made perhaps the greatest contribution of all.*

AFFIRMATION: I place a high value on myself.

HOT FLASH: Give yourself the credit you deserve.

—MAUREEN C.

"If there's one thing I'd want to say to other women in midlife, it would be, start giving yourself more value," says Maureen, age fifty. "Whatever you've done, whether you've been a mother, a wife, a corporate executive, or a starving artist, be proud of it and don't let *anyone* take that away!"

Successfully navigating the Change of Life requires our willingness to place a higher value on who we are and all we've accomplished. Doing so isn't self-aggrandizing. In fact self-respect is a humbling and courageous first step toward claiming our own humanity.

Are you placing a high enough value on your-self? Have you given yourself credit and respect for everything you've achieved in the course of forty or fifty years?

In this final exercise throw away your modesty and complete the following sentence:

I am a valuable person in so many ways. Here are a few examples:

Knowing our own value is the key to empower-ment. Make this a daily affirmation. Live as if you mean it.

*I was to be joining an ancient sisterhood. A medicine
hoop of age and wisdom.*

—MARIGOLD FINE

In midlife we claim membership in an ancient circle of feminine power, symbolized by the medicine hoop.

It is an honor to have reached this point; we join hands and hearts, combining our communal wisdom, nurturing one another, connected by a sense of universal compassion and love.

We have each done our fair share of struggling, learning, and healing in order to have earned the right to place ourselves within this holy circle of crones.

AFFIRMATION: I belong here.

STRIVING

There is a mountaintop with enough room for all of us.
—MARIANNE WILLIAMSON

"There cannot be too many glorious women. There cannot be too much success," concludes Marianne Williamson, in her book *A Woman's Worth*.

I concur. And I invite you—and you—and you—and every woman to open your eyes, see the vistas, and begin the long climb to the top of the mountain. Where our splendor is visible from every peak. Where choices are plentiful, differences are respected, and every possibility is within arm's reach. Where we can see backward and forward and even a bit of heaven as we continue to come more fully, more gloriously, more ecstatically into our own.

AFFIRMATION: I see the mountaintop.

INDEX